I0143489

GHOST INVESTIGATOR

Volume II:
From Gettysburg, PA to Lizzie Borden, AX

Written by
Linda Zimmermann

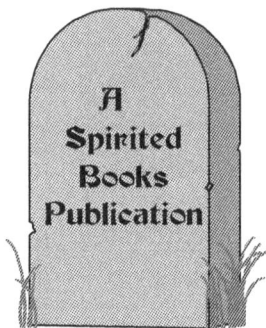

A
Spirited
Books
Publication

Also by Linda Zimmermann

Bad Astronomy
Forging A Nation
Civil War Memories
Ghosts of Rockland County
Haunted Hudson Valley
More Haunted Hudson Valley
Haunted Hudson Valley III
A Funny Thing Happened on the Way to Gettysburg
Rockland County: Century of History
Mind Over Matter
Home Run
Ghost Investigator, Volume 1: Hauntings of the Hudson Valley

The author is always looking for new ghost stories. If you would like to share a haunting experience go to:

www.ghostinvestigator.com

Or write to:

Linda Zimmermann
P.O. Box 192
Blooming Grove, NY 10914

Or send email to:
lindazim@frontiernet.net

Cover Art by Gordon Bond: tpoastro@hotmail.com

Ghost Investigator
Volume 2: From Gettysburg, PA to Lizzie Borden, AX
Copyright © 2002 Linda Zimmermann

ISBN: 0-9712326-1-X

Introduction

For several years now, I have been writing about haunted places in the Hudson Valley region of New York and New Jersey. On occasion, I've had to stretch that regional envelope as opportunities for investigations came up in other locations. Although there are still a few stories from the Hudson Valley in *Ghost Investigator, Volume 2: Gettysburg, PA to Lizzie Borden, AX*, the title makes it clear that I've officially expanded my territory.

There are just too many ghosts out there to be limited to any one area. In fact, I'm still amazed at the sheer number and scope of haunted houses, cemeteries, businesses, ships, roads, and just about anything else you can name. In the future, I plan to seek out the hauntings offering the most compelling evidence, regardless of where they may be.

The stories in this book are indeed compelling—from terrified babysitters in a private home, to a vast battlefield, and from a prison that held murderers, to the house where two of the most famous unsolved murders were committed. This is also the first book in which I have personally investigated every location. As always, I present an honest account of what did, or did not, happen there. Evidence is always open for different interpretations, and readers are encouraged to form their own opinions based upon that evidence, as well as their own common sense.

One question I am asked on a regular basis is, "Where can I go to see a ghost?"

Well, if it were that simple, I wouldn't need to keep searching for proof of the existence of ghosts. Actual apparitions are one of the most rare manifestations of a haunting, so you may want to decrease your expectation level to something like cold spots, footsteps or psychic impressions. That being said, I regularly hear eyewitness accounts of phantom figures appearing to skeptics who weren't even looking for them. So then, where do you go to see a ghost?

This book contains stories about two prime locations—Gettysburg, Pennsylvania, and Lizzie Borden's house in Fall River, Massachusetts. If you are unable to travel that far, check your area's newspapers around Halloween, when stories of local hauntings often appear. There are also books and many Internet sites that list haunted places by state. Local historical societies and libraries may also be able to help. If you do find information on a potentially haunted site, just make sure you don't trespass, and please respect the privacy of home and land owners.

Another word of caution—be sure you are prepared to deal with the possibility of finding what you are looking for. A personal encounter with a nasty spirit just might be more than you can handle. In the comfort and security of your own home, it's easy to believe you will be fearless. However, the reality of standing alone in the damp and darkness of a prison cell, in the uneasy silence of an isolated cemetery, or within the musty, confining walls of an old basement, is a different story.

What would you do if you were suddenly engulfed by an icy cold mass of air? How would you react if you were at the scene of a murder and a door opened on its own? Where would you run if phantom footsteps approached you, and you had the sickening feeling that something wanted to harm you?

Perhaps it's best that you just keep reading about haunted places, with all of the lights on, in the safety of your own home. There's no sense risking your mind, body and soul seeking out spirits of the dead. After all, that's what ghost investigators are for…

Contents

Acknowledgements

I would like to thank the wonderful staff at the Lizzie Borden Bed & Breakfast Museum for their valuable assistance in gathering information.

To Thomas Ellis, the deepest gratitude from all concerned for "clearing" up two of the cases in this book.

To all of the people who were kind enough to let me into their homes to conduct investigations, many thanks for your courage, enthusiasm and patience.

And to Bob, special thanks for always being there, and for those hand-labeled floor plans that would have been unreadable if I had done them.

Please Note:

When only first names or fictitious names (introduced in quotation marks) are used, and specific addresses are not listed, it is to protect the privacy of the individuals and their property. It's bad enough being haunted by ghosts—these people don't need to be haunted by curiosity seekers as well!

Home Invasion

Everyone loves a scary story about a terrorized babysitter—except, of course, the babysitter herself. The homeowner usually isn't too thrilled, either. The following story is just such a case, and it will certainly make you think twice about spending the night in a strange house—even when that house appears to be just like any other in your neighborhood.

*

In February of 2001, the "Grant" family moved into a house in Spring Valley, New York. The high ranch was built in 1960 and was in a quiet, well-manicured development. By September, however, a member of the family had an experience that shattered their short-lived ideal of the tranquil, suburban home. From that point, a string of bizarre and terrifying events began to take place that would test the family's strong Christian beliefs.

In February of 2002, "Marilyn Grant", a nurse in a local hospital, sent me an e-mail message with the title "Urgent Help Needed!!" She explained that she had read *Ghosts of Rockland County* and was having some problems similar to those I described in the book. She went on to write that, "four babysitters all had the same experience in the same room," and asked if I would be interested in investigating. This tantalizingly brief description certainly caught my attention, and I immediately contacted her for more information.

After speaking with Marilyn, I felt that this was a situation that needed a psychic with the ability to perform a clearing. Marilyn was somewhat desperate to rid her home of what appeared to be several spirits, so we tried to arrange a meeting at her house with a psychic from New Jersey. However, getting three busy people together proved to be as difficult as catching an apparition on film, and when a particularly frightening episode occurred at the Grant home on the night of April 29, 2002, I decided to visit the next day by myself.

I arrived at the house around 6pm and was greeted by Marilyn's aunt, who had lived with the family on and off since they moved in. She explained that Marilyn was not back from work yet, but would be home at any minute. I stepped inside with some trepidation, fully aware that very unpleasant things happened inside that house. As I later told Marilyn, you would think I would be used to this sort of thing by now, but how do you "get used" to encountering the unknown? Especially when that unknown has proven to be malicious and has attacked several women.

Some psychics and mediums have told me that nothing frightens them and they have no hesitation going up against the nastiest entities the spirit world can dish out. However, I tend to agree with the old saying, "Fools rush in." I prefer to walk, carefully.

The house was a typical high ranch with the front door opening to a landing with a short flight of stairs leading downstairs to two rooms of living space on the right and the garage on the left. Another short flight of stairs leads up to the main floor with the open living/dining room area on the right, the kitchen straight ahead and the bedrooms to the left. As I was carrying the bags of equipment downstairs into the television room, I felt a disturbing chill, but just then Marilyn's car pulled into the driveway so I went back up to greet her.

Part of my job of investigating a haunting is to judge the character and veracity of eyewitnesses. Often, this is the only evidence I have to go on, so it is crucial for me to be able to distinguish between those who have truly encountered the unknown, and those who simply have a really vivid imagination (while they are not mutually exclusive, it is easier to deal with the former than the latter). I immediately felt comfortable with Marilyn and knew that her professional training makes her an excellent observer. She also maintains a deep faith which gives her both comfort and strength.

"Now that I think about it," Marilyn said once I got the tape recorder started, "At the closing I was discussing my religious beliefs with the women who sold us the house. She said it was a good thing, because I would need a strong faith to live here. I really had no idea what she could have meant at the time."

The previous owner had lived in the house for 13 years, and during that time her marriage ended in a very painful divorce, and many other "negative" things had happened to her which she didn't care to discuss. She wondered out loud if all the bad things occurred after moving in because she never had the house blessed. She then looked at Marilyn and insisted, "You make sure you bless this house!"

As Marilyn related the story to me, we were sitting on the couch in the downstairs television room, and her aunt was facing us on a loveseat to our left. The tape recorder sat on the sofa between us and I noticed it stopping briefly a couple of times. Although the batteries were freshly recharged that afternoon, I asked Marilyn to hold off speaking for a moment while I plugged the tape recorder into an outlet. However, the mysterious problem continued throughout our conversation. In fact, at one point when I was asking about cold spots, the recorder turned itself on and off several times in rapid succession. When I played back the tape the next day, you can actually hear the distinctive distortion sound of the tape being stopped and started.

The malfunctioning tape recorder was becoming a real distraction, which I certainly didn't need. I was trying to pay attention to Marilyn and take notes, while keeping one eye on the recorder to make sure it was working. As I was determined to continue without these interruptions, I shut off the tape recorder and said to Marilyn that if something was trying to get our attention it had succeeded. I then said that hopefully it would leave us alone so I could get the rest of her story. Once I started the tape recorder again, there were no more problems. Skeptics would call this a coincidence. I consider it lucky that my words had the desired effect, and didn't annoy whatever it was causing the odd malfunction!

Marilyn related how the bizarre activity in the house first began. About six months after moving in, around late August or early September, her Aunt was sleeping in the room downstairs, next to the television room on the back side of the house when something terrifying and inexplicable happened.

"She looked petrified," Marilyn explained. "When I looked into her face it was not the person I knew. I had never seen her so afraid. She said, 'Marilyn, you need to do something about this house. Something is not right here.' Then she told me what had happened."

While she was sleeping, her aunt had terrible nightmares about other people in the house—in particular, a man who had a very overpowering presence. Waking up from what she thought was only a dream, she *physically* felt this male presence on top of her. It was a very real and very frightening attack, and it would only be the first of many.

Soon after this shocking experience, Marilyn began feeling like she was constantly being watched. She and her husband both saw shadowy figures moving from the kitchen and going downstairs. It would feel unnaturally cold some times, particularly in "The Room", as they came to call the downstairs bedroom. Even though they never mentioned these things to their two children (eight-year-old twins, a boy and a girl), they also appeared to have experienced several unusual things.

Marilyn explained that her daughter was the more vocal of the two children, and that her son was more likely not to express himself. While he had never outwardly spoken about anything strange, one night as he was entering the bathroom, he froze at the doorway and stared straight ahead. He wouldn't say what he saw, but he also wouldn't step inside the bathroom that night.

Soon after the first attack in The Room, Marilyn's daughter came to her in the downstairs TV room and asked, "Mommy, do we have someone living in the basement?"

"We don't have a basement. We have a room, here," Marilyn explained, pointing to the bedroom on the other side of the wall.

"You mean *below* the TV room," her daughter insisted, pointing to the floor under which was only solid ground.

"No," Marilyn replied a bit concerned. "Right here, *next* to this room."

3

The child then simply laughed and walked away.

"It was like someone was speaking through her," Marilyn said with a shudder. "I don't want to imagine that, but it scared me."

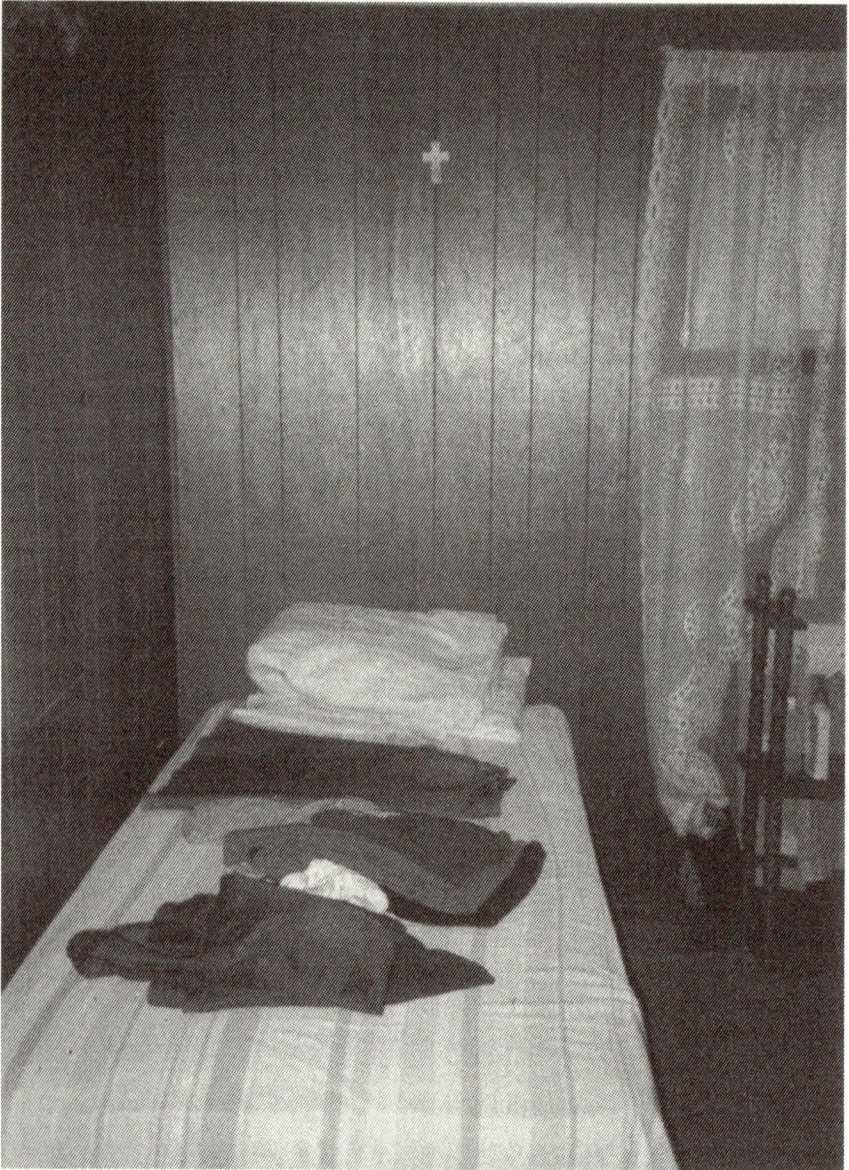

The room where the attacks occurred.

Another evening she heard her daughter scream and went into her bedroom to see what was the matter. Her daughter said she had seen a blue facemask with red bloody teeth. While children often imagine things, Marilyn explained that her daughter was very mature and intelligent for her age, and didn't make up things. This terrifying blue masked face was to show itself to her daughter on another occasion, and she was able to describe it exactly as it had appeared the first time.

While Marilyn never saw this mask, one thing everyone saw and couldn't get rid of was the disturbing painting on the wall of her son's room. One of the previous owners had painted a large, black, reclining skeletal figure on the wall, and numerous coats of paint failed to conceal it.

"Every time I paint over it, the image comes back. My son is terrified of it, so I finally had to get this bookshelf to conceal it," Marilyn said as she slid back the shelf so I could photograph the image. She has no idea why this skeleton was on the wall, and why the realtor didn't have the previous owners remove it before trying to sell the house.

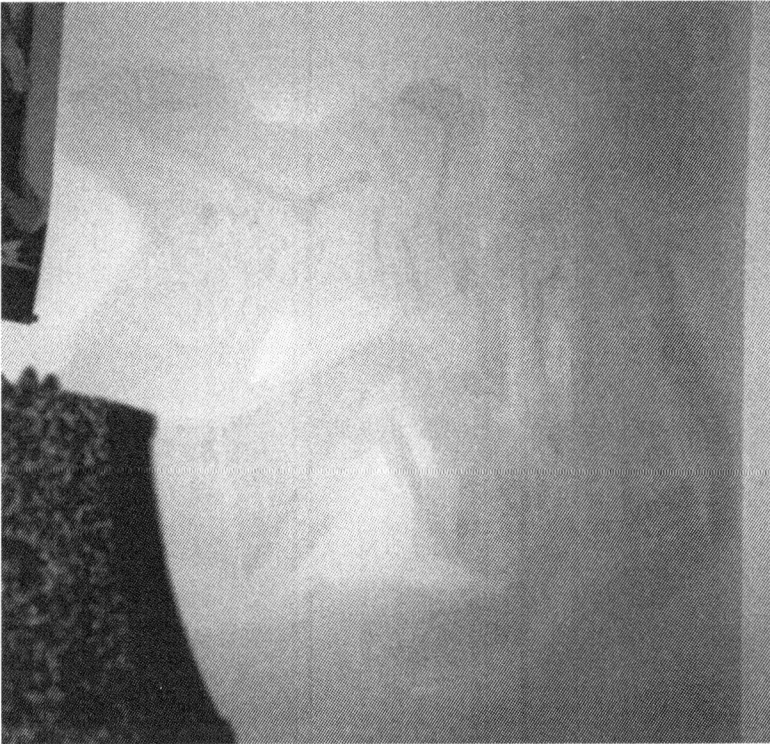

The figure of the skeleton keeps reappearing
despite several coats of paint.

Since Marilyn is often on the night shift at the hospital, it was nice to have her aunt living with them to help take care of the children. However, at the end of 2001, her aunt went back to Jamaica to spend some time with family there. After searching for a suitable sleep-in nanny, Marilyn found a woman who came highly recommended and was very enthusiastic about the position. The woman needed work and Marilyn needed a nanny, so it seemed like an ideal situation. Except for one small thing…

Not wanting to scare the woman, Marilyn did not mention any of the house's more unusual aspects, hoping that whatever it was would leave the new resident alone. Unfortunately, almost immediately the new nanny began complaining of banging noises in The Room where she slept. She described the sounds as being like something heavy striking an iron pipe. Even though Marilyn suggested that it was probably just the heating or water pipes in the walls, she knew that in fact, there were no pipes.

The nanny also began having terrible nightmares about another family in the house, and she said that she felt as if someone was trying to get on top of her in the middle of the night. After only two weeks the nanny quit. As much as she needed a job, this was more than her nerves could stand.

Once again, Marilyn began searching. This time she found a woman who was pregnant, and was thrilled at the prospect of a comfortable room in a nice house. She moved in on a Friday night and moved out the first thing Monday morning. She claimed that someone was trying to get on top of her in the middle of the night.

There were to be a total of four babysitters who left in rapid succession, due to the disturbing activities in The Room.

Another person who had no prior knowledge of the house had strange experiences. A male nurse who worked with Marilyn also did home improvement as a side job. As he was working on remodeling the upstairs bathroom, he said it sounded like someone kept snapping his fingers at him, as if trying to get his attention. The repeated snapping sound certainly had the desired effect and the man became convinced the house was haunted.

When the aunt's daughter came for a visit, she had strange dreams about a strange man and a woman in the house. One afternoon while she was there, they all heard a loud smashing sound, as if a large glass object had been shattered on the floor. Searching the house from top to bottom, they never discovered a single piece of broken glass, or anything else that could have accounted for the noise. Then there were the footsteps, creaking doors and floorboards, all occurring when none of the living inhabitants of the house were moving about.

A female friend at the hospital, who knew nothing of what went on in Marilyn's house, told her one day that she thought it was odd that she had a dream about the house. She said that there was another family there. There was a very stern and domineering father who ruled his family and household, a slender wife, a blond girl about seven to ten years old, a boy and a dog. In her dream the father was very annoyed that Marilyn's family was in *his* house and wanted her family out of there.

A month after moving in, Marilyn's pastor had blessed the house. As that blessing was apparently unsuccessful, she now sought the help of a local Catholic priest. Marilyn explained to the priest's secretary that she needed help, that something very disturbing was happening in her home, that she had strong Christian beliefs, and even though she wasn't Catholic, she hoped the priest would be able to help. The priest never contacted her and never offered any help.

When Marilyn's aunt returned from Jamaica, they decided to take matters into their own hands. At about 10:45pm one night, they began a series of prayers and rituals they hoped would rid the house of the unwanted spirits. Unfortunately, at least one spirit didn't appreciate the attempted eviction, as some unseen force began violently kicking the sliding doors (leading to the outside) next to The Room. It clearly sounded like someone kicking the outer screens of the large glass doors, as if trying to get into the house. Marilyn and her aunt did not continue with the rituals.

All of this convinced the Grants that something had to be done. Since the clergy seemed either unable or unwilling to help, Marilyn contacted me in February of 2002 to see if I knew of any psychics who could bring peace and quiet to the house. As I mentioned, we were hoping a psychic would join us at the house, but Marilyn could no longer wait after what occurred the last week of April.

One evening, she and her husband were watching television downstairs when the washing machine, which was in a utility room by the garage, suddenly came on by itself. All that week Marilyn had trouble sleeping, waking up every hour. Then one night as her aunt sat on the couch downstairs, she underwent another intense and terrifying attack by an unseen male presence who tried to force his way on top of her.

The next day I arrived. In addition to my tape recorder starting and stopping, both my digital and 35mm cameras refused to work several times when I tried to photograph The Room. I finally did manage to get several pictures, but numerous times I pressed the shutter release buttons and nothing happened. Both cameras worked fine before I arrived (I check every piece of equipment before an investigation) and they worked with no problem in the rest of the house. There were also high EMF (electromagnetic field) readings in The Room. A few times on the stairs and in the kitchen and living room there were high readings, but they came and went as if something was passing through.

As Marilyn gave me a tour of the upstairs, in the area between the living and dining room we distinctly heard a loud sneezing or "shushing" sound just a few feet behind or backs. We immediately turned to find the source. Marilyn's aunt was right behind us and we both said, "God bless you." She put up her hands and shook her head and said, "That wasn't me!" As we went into the kitchen, we heard the sound again, only a few feet away from

7

us. It was loud and sharp, and either intended to simply distract us, or get us to be quiet. (It is interesting to note that one woman who had stayed in the house said she had dreamt that a schoolteacher and two male students were in the house. The "shushing" sounds would certainly be in keeping with a teacher trying to quiet her unruly students!)

As I drove home from Marilyn's house (in a very nasty thunderstorm, I might add), I went over in my mind everything that had transpired. Here was a case were numerous credible and independent witnesses with no prior knowledge all had the same experiences. Electronic equipment malfunctioned. There were inexplicable sounds and cold spots. Most disturbing, however, was that this classic haunting was not friendly or even benign—it was dark, negative and potentially harmful. This was not just a curiosity, it was something that needed to be dealt with quickly and decisively. As it didn't look likely that we would be able to get a psychic on the scene any time soon, I immediately looked for alternatives.

In March of 2002, I was the guest on the popular radio program *Coast to Coast with Art Bell*. The show ran from 2am to 6am EST (way past my usual bedtime!), and by 7am that morning when I checked my email I already had several screens full of messages. It was impossible to respond to all of them, but I did my best and made note of a few which were of particular interest. One such message was from Thomas Ellis, in Ohio, who explained that he performed remote house clearings; i.e., he didn't need to actually go to a site to work on it. Realizing I would be skeptical, he offered to do a test case on any place I selected. All I needed to tell him was please check on "House A," without providing any other details or information.

Of course, I was skeptical, but Marilyn was also desperate, so the week before I visited the house I emailed Thomas and let him know that I wanted him to check on a location, but not to perform any clearing yet. That was all I told him. As there could be absolutely no prior knowledge about the case, anything Thomas would find could not have been influenced by anything I revealed. What he said would be what he found.

On April 24, Thomas sent a report on his findings. It was a long and detailed report, and he took the time to explain his terms and references. Some of his findings are as follows:

The property (house, grounds, buildings, animals, items, etc.) contains:

4 Wandering Soul Entities: 3 females, 1 male. Relates to prior owners. One girl is 7-10 years old. The wandering souls are not really negative, but are annoying as they suppose that the present owner is encroaching on their property. None are of American Indian descent, although I get the impression that several have been on the property over 200 years. Depending upon the age of the home, it is possible

8

that they predated when it was built and that they were affiliated with another dwelling there or were buried on the property somewhere.

2 Shadow Beings—entities—that are from a parallel world/dimension and can barely be seen clearly—brings much negativity.

Thomas' report went on to say that there was also a substantial amount of negative energy in many different forms that had been in the property prior to the building of the house, and had been intensifying over the years. Such negative energy could provoke altercations and friction between the people living there. The bottom line was that this was not a healthy environment in which to live.

The good news, if there can be such a thing in such cases, was that all of this could be cleared away. All Thomas needed was for Marilyn to say the word.

Of course, I didn't quite know what to make of all this before I visited the house, but once I had experienced it for myself and listened to Marilyn's story, several things stood out.

- Several people had claimed that they felt another family was in the house, and one woman had even specifically stated that there was a girl, 7-10 years old, exactly as Thomas described her.
- These claims had also stressed that this phantom family felt that Marilyn's family was intruding on *their* property.
- The area was once inhabited by American Indians, and it is possible that subsequent colonists and farmers had once lived on the property.
- Marilyn's daughter had insisted that there were people *under* the house.
- Both Marilyn and her husband saw shadow-like figures in the house on several occasions.
- The previous owner had complained that her life had fallen apart while living in the house, with a divorce and many "negative" things occurring.

Based upon all of the evidence, I suggested to Marilyn that she allow Thomas to clear the house. She agreed, and from halfway across the country, Thomas Ellis attempted to remove the entities and negative energy from Marilyn's home. While the initial process would be completed in a single day, Thomas explained that it would take a couple of weeks to make sure everything was gone, with periodic check-ups to make sure nothing had returned.

The results? For two weeks there were no strange occurrences in the house—which given its recent history was something of a record. Then a few things did occur, but none of which appeared malicious. A new babysitter heard the sound of a key in the front door and heard footsteps, but no one was there. The next morning Marilyn heard a child run downstairs, drop a ball, and say "Good-bye." While this would not usually be a strange thing in a house with two children, her daughter had already left for school and her son was still fast asleep!

Marilyn informed Thomas of these events and he thought that perhaps they were just some positive spirits passing through, and he would periodically check on the house and make sure nothing was making any long term plans to stay.

While skeptics would undoubtedly have a field day with this case, it would be disingenuous of them to attribute everything that happened to imagination or the power of suggestion. The undeniable facts remain that numerous people who had previously known nothing of the house and its dark intruders all described the same invisible male attacking them, heard the same type of sounds and sensed the same presences.

Hopefully, the nightmare of this Spring Valley family is now over. Thanks to their prayers and determination, and the compassionate work of Thomas Ellis, they may now experience nothing but happiness and tranquility, as might the unhappy and negative entities which once lived there. While it can't be stated with certainty that all of the haunting activity in the house has ceased forever, it might do well to have some faith.

After all, it was faith that gave Marilyn and her family the strength to endure this ordeal.

Thomas Ellis can be contacted through: www.transformationsbythomas.com

An Evening on Death Row

The week between Christmas and New Year's Day is usually one of celebrations and parties. However, if you happen to be a ghost investigator it's the perfect time to get locked in an abandoned prison and spend the night sitting on death row.

Well…it seemed like a good idea at the time!

The story actually begins in October of 2001, when I was doing a book signing at the *Headless Horseman Haunted House and Hayride* in Ulster Park, New York. This is a first-rate event that scares the daylights out of thousands of people each Halloween season. If you have never been there, I highly recommend it.

I was seated at a table near the area where people climbed onto the hay trucks and were taken deep into the woods, and throughout the night I could hear their distant screams. The moon was bright, that autumn crispness was in the air and it was the perfect night for a good ghost story. While I was the one telling most of the ghost stories, several people told me some frightening tales of their own encounters. Often, these stories involve places that aren't available for hands-on research, such as houses that have been torn down, or have been sold to people who don't look favorably on paranormal investigations in their living rooms. Fortunately, there was one story that night which not only sounded fascinating, it sounded like the ideal place for a visit—an old, abandoned prison where the tortured spirits of dead inmates still terrorize the living.

A man asked if I had ever heard of Eastern State Penitentiary in Philadelphia, Pennsylvania. While the name rang a bell, I couldn't recall any specific details. He said his brother works for the secret service and that the government officially considers only two places in the country to be haunted. One of those places is Eastern State. (No, he didn't know what that other place was.)

He went on to say that a few years ago, during some repair work on the prison, a group of workmen ran out and refused to go back to inside because of all the frightening and inexplicable things that occurred. He also said that there were plans to demolish the place, but that it was so haunted they were afraid to tear it down.

Now I know this sounds like the plot of an *X-Files* show, or the ravings of a lunatic, but it also sounded just wild enough to have some truth behind it. It was at least worth a trip on the internet.

The next day I went to www.easternstate.com, and to my delight, found an excellent web site that offered a 360-degree virtual tour of the various cellblocks and buildings. There was no mention of ghosts on the site, but the actual history of the place was enough to curl your hair.

11

Prior to the 19th century, jails were basically large open rooms where all of the prisoners (men, women and even children) were held together. Generally, the prisoners would be kept there on a more or less a temporary basis until they received some type of physical punishment, e.g., whipping, hanging, etc. However, some citizens who professed to be more enlightened felt that such cruel punishments should be stopped, and they sought a more compassionate way to deal with prisoners. In 1787, a group of influential men in Philadelphia met at the home of Benjamin Franklin to discuss plans for a new facility.

Calling themselves *The Philadelphia Society for Alleviating the Miseries of Public Prisons*, they proposed an innovative design—a prison where each man was to be kept in complete isolation in his own cell. By having absolutely no contact or communication with another living soul, the designers felt that the prisoner would have no choice but to reflect upon his crime, realize the error of his ways and ultimately become penitent—hence the new term penitentiary. It was an idea that sounded marvelous to the gentlemen who discussed it over cigars and brandy after dinner, but to the inmates who would spend years completely alone, it was a torture as cruel and insidious as any medieval device.

A wooden model of the original prison.
Photo courtesy of Sam Rizzo III.

In 1829, the long awaited Eastern State Penitentiary began operations on open farmland about a mile from the city of Philadelphia. At the time, it was the most expensive building ever constructed in the United States, and it boasted features that not even the White House contained—flush toilets, central heating and running water. This was truly the first modern building in the country, and tourists from across the United States and from around the world came to see this wonder of new thought and new design.

While many tourists sang the praises of this revolutionary penitentiary, one visitor saw it for what it really was—a place that drove inmates to the depth of despair and insanity. In 1842, author Charles Dickens wrote, "In its intention I am well convinced that it is kind, humane, and meant for reformation; but I am persuaded that those who designed this system of Prison Discipline, and those benevolent gentleman who carry it into execution, do not know what it is that they are doing...I hold this slow and daily tampering with the mysteries of the brain to be immeasurably worse than any torture of the body."

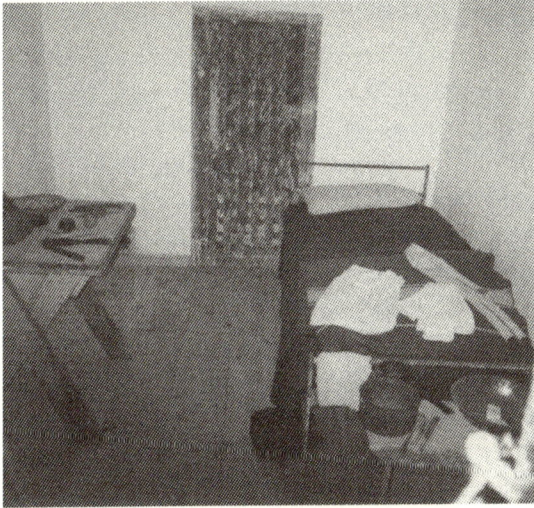

A cell restored to its original appearance.

A cell as it looks today after years of deterioration.
Photo courtesy of Sam Rizzo III.

Prisoners had no contact with one another or with the outside world. They ate, worked and exercised in their own cells. If they needed to be moved to another location, hoods were placed over their heads so that they could not even see the guards, or where they were going. Inmates endured years of this silent isolation. Death seemed to be a blessed escape from the madness that resulted from this allegedly compassionate path to penitence.

However, as powerful men continued to perceive this to be a brilliant system, over 300 penitentiaries were constructed around the world based upon Eastern State. The long blocks of private cells radiating from a central rotunda became the standard of prison design, and the Quaker-based concept of the Pennsylvania System of isolation and work spread across the globe.

Eventually, however, the Pennsylvania System slowly eroded. The need for more space led to placing more than one prisoner in a cell, and pressure from human rights advocates finally brought about the official demise of the system in 1913. Prisoners were allowed to speak to one another, have visitors, and basically be treated like human beings.

Yet, as cruel as this system had been, it can't be forgotten that the people who were incarcerated there were far from innocent. The inmates at Eastern State constituted the worst examples of mankind—murderers, rapists and the criminally insane. Arguments still rage as to how to treat such people, with one side insisting that cable television in every cell is hardly punishment, and the other extreme claiming that no crime deserves anything as harsh as the death penalty. For Eastern State, the argument resolved itself in 1971, when the decaying prison was officially closed.

In the 1980s, the old penitentiary was slated to be demolished to make way for a new development, but several groups successfully petitioned for preservation. In 1994, Eastern State reopened—this time strictly for tourists. Today the site is operated by a non-profit organization, and in addition to its regular tours, hosts other special events. One the most popular is a Halloween tour called *Terror Behind the Walls*, with great special effects and real people jumping out of dark corners to scare you.

Like the place needs real people to do that…

After reading up on Eastern State Penitentiary, I e-mailed fellow ghost investigator Mike Worden to see if he was up for a field trip. As he is a former corrections officer and a current police officer, I kidded him that if there were any ghosts, they would love to get their phantom hands on him! Mike was all for the trip (although he did feel like he would be going in there wearing a very large bulls-eye), so he made some phone calls and arranged a private tour. However, as the facility was officially closed for the winter, and we would need to hire a guide, it wasn't going to be cheap, but where else can you rent an entire abandoned penitentiary for the night?

This would be one occasion where we could comfortably accommodate a large group, so I invited some friends who had been anxious to go on a real ghost hunt. I had also wanted a psychic to come along, as I imagined this place would be a symphony of psychic impressions, although the term maelstrom would probably be a more appropriate term than symphony. Due to the time of year and previous commitments, several friends and the psychic were unable to attend, but there would be six of us spending the night in jail.

The "gang" would be comprised of me and my boyfriend Bob Strong, Mike and his friend Autumn, and 15-year-old ghost enthusiast Sam Rizzo III and his father Richard Koestler. In addition to a varied career in science,

Richard is also an Emergency Medical Technician. Considering we would be wandering around crumbling structures in the dark, and encountering who knows what, it was a comforting thought knowing an EMT would be there.

Bob and I hit a lot of traffic on the New Jersey Turnpike on the way to Philly, but as we allowed extra time, we still arrived at the penitentiary about half an hour before our scheduled 4pm meeting with our guide. The city that once was a mile away, now engulfs the towering fortress-like walls of Eastern State, but it nonetheless makes a striking first impression as its massive stone towers first come into view. Now in a neighborhood of small apartment buildings, restaurants and gas stations, the shear size of the old jail is still intimidating.

One of the medieval-looking towers.

We circumnavigated the outside walls and took pictures of the dark, foreboding towers against the bright blue winter sky. We were glad it wasn't snowing or raining, but the previously unseasonably mild temperatures were forecast to be more seasonable that night, i.e., cold—one thing I can't stand. I put on so many layers of clothing they restricted my movements, but being an amateur astronomer and having spent many long, cold nights observing, I knew that as long as you could still walk, lean over, and hold a flashlight, there was no such thing as too many clothes. I also had a thermos of hot tea in reserve, but I did bemoan the fact that I didn't have an extension cord long enough to bring my electric blanket around the prison.

The imposing stone walls of Eastern state Penitentiary.

Mike and Autumn soon arrived, and Sammy and Richard were right behind them. Our guide, Brian, was right on schedule and we placed ourselves in his knowledgeable hands. Rumor had it that it wasn't the safest neighborhood (a car on he street with broken windows confirmed that), so we were relieved to find that we could park inside the prison. In fact, as Brian pulled a heavy chain to open the massive gates, he explained that he would be locking the doors behind us. It seemed ironic that the safest place in the neighborhood was now the inside of the prison. Of course, safe was a relative term...

After bringing in all the cars and locking ourselves in, we filled out release forms stating that we were aware of all the potential risks. As the prison had fallen into disrepair decades earlier, there was a lot of debris throughout the facility. Most of the cellblocks had no electricity, and therefore no lights. There was no mention on the forms of any paranormal dangers, but there were enough in the solid physical world to keep you on your toes.

Brian also issued us walkie-talkies, and although we had brought a couple of pairs for ourselves, his would allow us to be in contact with him at any point. As members of our group might decide to split up during the night, and he would not be with us at all times, it was a wise precaution if anyone needed assistance. There was also the possibility of someone panicking who would need to get out as soon as possible.

Our ghost investigating squad at the start of our prison stay:
Bob, me, Autumn, Mike, Sammy and Richard.

In the fading light, Brian began a general tour around the prison complex. I feel it is always best to scout out a site in daylight so you can acquaint yourself with all the nooks and crannies, find the best places to set up equipment and check for objects that might appear unusual it the darkness. A hanging light fixture, a bit of shiny metal or pieces of fabric could produce images that might be misinterpreted if you don't know exactly what you were looking at. (An amusing example of this was at the Trolley View farm, when something in the basement momentarily made my heart stop. See page 52.)

At one spot outside on the dirt ground of a former exercise yard, my EMF meter registered an unnaturally high reading, which was confirmed by Mike's meter. Unless there were some kind of underground electric cables at that spot, there didn't appear to be any apparent reason for the readings. The area in question was roughly a couple of yards in diameter, and the EMF field did not trail away the farther away you went, it abruptly ended at a definitive perimeter. I asked if the location had any significance, and Brian mentioned that the adjacent cellblock had been the scene of violent riots, but he was unaware of any particular incidents occurring exactly on that spot of ground outside. Even more curious, when we returned later on that night, the electromagnetic field we had measured had disappeared. Chalk one up for the ghosts of Eastern State Penitentiary.

The area of the yard that had the mysterious electromagnetic field.

After getting our bearings on the ground, we wanted to see how things looked from above, so we headed for the warden's building, which also contained a guard's tower. With all the misery and violence that had transpired in the cellblocks over the years, I didn't consider the administration building to be an area likely to have significant paranormal activity, but it was actually in the warden's offices that I felt the first unmistakable signs that something was there. It wasn't anything that registered on my meters or cameras, but my "internal sensors" were ringing loud and clear. Though I try to conduct objective, scientific investigations, it would be foolish to ignore my intuition, which has served me well throughout my life. (Of course, it might have served me even better if I had listened to it more often!)

I can't stress enough that everyone has intuitive powers. Whether you prefer to call it a sixth sense, being psychic or just a "gut feel," it is simply a matter of paying attention to that little voice inside of you and appreciating and cultivating it. However, as much as I value my intuition, I do realize it is subjective, and do not consider that it provides hard scientific proof. It is an unknown variable in the mysterious equation of life, but if there is one thing

I learned from my years as a research scientist it's this: just because you don't understand or can't quantify the nature of a thing, it doesn't mean it does not exist.

What I felt was not anything that was menacing or frightening, but it was persistent and strong. As we walked around the abandoned offices, with glass and debris crunching under the sturdy soles of our hiking boots, I felt as if someone was simply trying to communicate his presence to me. As we all moved to the staircase that led to the guard tower, I felt as if I didn't want to go up there, that I needed to stay in those rooms alone. However, as I wanted a birds-eye view of the place, I started up the staircase anyway.

It was very dark, very narrow and very steep. Brian went first, Bob was next and I was behind him, but after each step I felt more strongly that I shouldn't go up there. I should point out that I have no fear of heights (in fact, I enjoy them, and later on that night I did go to the top of another guard tower and felt fine), and I have been in tight caves and coal mines and didn't experience claustrophobia.

This was something different. While the last thing a ghost investigator wants to do is appear to be a wimp, after about a dozen steps I stopped climbing and went back down. Everyone else went to the top of the tower, which turned out to be a very high platform with a very low wall, which caused more than one member of the group to feel somewhat unnerved. They remained up there for a few minutes taking pictures, and I took the time to walk quietly through the old offices and corridors.

In the silence the presence grew stronger. I could almost hear him, almost picture him—like an

The tower that contained the warden's offices, which rises over the front gate.
Photo courtesy of Sam Rizzo III.

19

elusive word perched on the tip of your tongue. I spoke to him silently with private words I use to urge whatever spirits may be trapped or confused to move on. Soon everyone began to descend the stairs and the mood was broken, but as I write this now, many months later, I can close my eyes and still recall that soothing, peaceful feeling of that brief encounter. It was good I had those moments, because that was to be last bit of tranquility I would experience that night.

Next stop—Death Row. It was one of the more modern buildings, consisting of two floors with two rows of cells placed back to back. Darkness had now fallen and only the dim light of some distant buildings revealed the bleak, stark lines of cells. Mike and I decided to set up our camcorders at opposite ends of the row on the western side of the top floor. I took the back wall, while he set up at the entrance. Our guide Brian remained outside, but I suggested that everyone else pick a cell and sit quietly while the cameras taped in infrared.

Even as I was setting up the camera, I could see on the viewscreen that there were several small, white spots moving around in front of me. As it was a dusty, dirty place, airborne particles might account for those spots, but dust couldn't account for everything that happened on death row that night.

This is most likely a massive understatement, but there is nothing quite like the feeling of sitting alone in the silent blackness of a death row cell in a cold, abandoned prison. You cannot help but experience the desolation and the hopelessness, and you cannot help but imagine the violence, cruelty and the perversity of the men who spent their final days on earth caged up in those small spaces.

These cells contained the worst examples humanity could offer—men who committed unspeakable atrocities, men who even in their last hours reached through those bars grasping at guards, hoping to kill one last victim before they themselves were executed. There were also those who realized the mistakes they had made, and lived every last minute in fear, desperation and anguish over the fate that awaited them. These cells once contained the greatest concentration of evil and torment, and it was in these cells that we sat, hearts pumping, minds racing, wondering what could happen.

Suddenly a motion detector alarm pierced the silence. It had been placed near the entrance and, as I was on the opposite end of the cellblock, I didn't know what was going on. When no one spoke after a few seconds, I leaned out of my cell and asked if anyone had walked past the motion detector. Mike was still behind his camera, and everybody else was still in their cells. A few specks of dust aren't sufficient to set off one of these detectors. There must be something solid and substantial to trigger the alarm, and it wasn't anyone in our group.

Sammy turned off the motion detector, and later told me that just before it was set off he felt something touch his ankle. Actually, it was more than something simply touching him—he said it felt as if a hand had momentarily grabbed his ankle. I give him credit for not screaming and running out of the place.

The Death Row cells.

After the detector incident, we decided to shift operations to the other side of the death row cellblock. This time, no one would be in the cells, and Mike and I decided to set up our cameras side by side, facing toward the back wall, with a view encompassing the entire width of that section. The few moving white lights I had taped in infrared on the first side began appearing in front of my camera again, only this time it was far more than a few isolated specks. It was like a sudden storm of tiny orbs surging in front of me—nothing we had ever seen before. Nothing appeared in the beams of our flashlights, and most unusual was the fact that Mike's camera did not record the same flood of objects.

Our camcorders are virtually identical—same manufacturer, same features, and they were set up at the same angle in the same direction just a couple of feet apart. So if there was dust blowing around, or some other natural phenomena, why did my camcorder see it, and his didn't? And, just as inexplicable, if it was some type of paranormal energy, why and how did it make its presence known to one camera, and not another right next to it?

And just to put the icing on the cake of this bizarre situation, the motion detector placed in front of us (aimed straight down the row of cells) went off again, without anyone seeing or taping anything that could have caused the triggering of the alarm.

All things considered, my experiences on death row in Eastern State Penitentiary will not soon be forgotten.

Our next objective was the hospital ward, a place of great suffering and death. It was also a place where there had been many reports of shadowy figures and strange occurrences. Brian went inside the hospital cellblock with us, and then decided to go get a cup of hot coffee while we set up and did some more taping. The cold was starting to get to me as well, despite the many layers of clothing, and my thoughts were turning to the thermos of hot tea that I had left in the car. However, my focus quickly snapped back to the investigation due to a loud sound we all heard.

Our camcorders were back to back—mine facing into the darkness leading to the central rotunda, and Mike's aimed toward the door we had entered from the outside. We were roughly in the center of the long hospital cellblock, all standing within a few feet of one another when suddenly there was a loud crashing or banging sound. It came from the direction of the outside door, but was clearly from *inside* the cellblock. The sound was recorded on both of our camcorders, as was my voice a few seconds later asking, "What was that?"

"It must be our guide," Mike replied.

"Brian?" I called out, and waited. Seconds ticked away with no response.

"Maybe that *wasn't* him," Mike finally said as we all exchanged glances.

Later when we exited the hospital cellblock, we found Brian sitting outside sipping his coffee.

"Was that you who made that loud crashing sound a while ago?" I asked.

"No, I thought it was you guys," he replied somewhat puzzled.

Brian went onto say that he was sitting just outside the door when he heard the sound inside the cellblock and just assumed that one of our group had knocked over something or had slammed one of the heavy cell doors. I assured him it wasn't anything we had done.

So, if it wasn't Brian, and it wasn't any of us, who or what had caused that sound?

After the strange noise, we continued taping and taking readings for a while. Mike taped what sounded like something growling in one of the cells. There were several darting white lights visible in infrared. Again, I considered that it was airborne particles causing the phenomena, but several acted highly unusual by moving in and out of individual cells, and one even appeared to go *through* a door. Bob caught several of these orb-like shapes with his digital camera, as did Sammy with his 35mm camera. After a few minutes of this

22

type of activity it seemed to stop, so we decided to pack up and move on to the central rotunda.

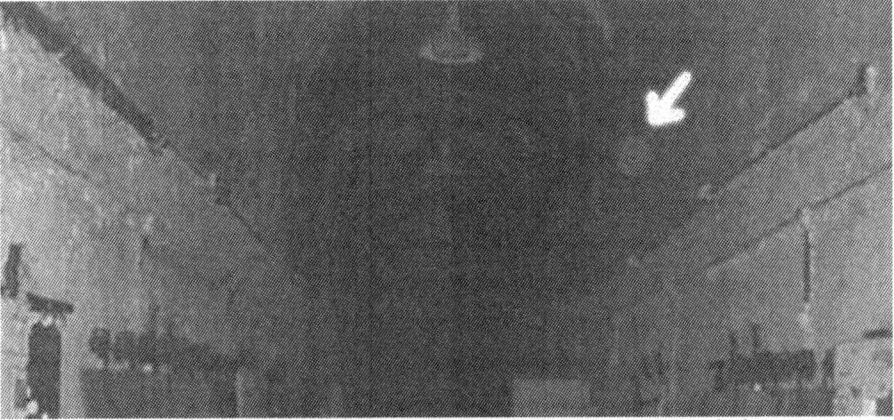

An orb in the hospital ward (above). The two pictures below
were taken several seconds apart and show the orb moving downward.
The last photo also has a few faint orbs by the doors on the right.

Spending hours navigating the dark labyrinth of passageways, buildings and courtyards was a bit disorienting, so it was somewhat reassuring to plant ourselves in the center of it all. We could appreciate the ingenious plan that created cellblocks radiating out from a central point like spokes of a wheel. This allowed just a few guards to be cognizant of what was occurring in the entire complex of cells, and if there was trouble you could access any point almost immediately.

We spent a few minutes trying to figure out the numbers of the cellblocks—as they were built at different times, they were numbered according to when they were built, not their clockwise order. (For example, cellblock 2 is between cellblocks 13 and 15.) Then we taped, photographed and took readings in each cellblock. Of particular interest from an historic perspective was the special cell on the rotunda that once held gangster Al Capone. However, his cell had not been as bleak as the average inmate—he had been allowed to furnish his cell with paintings, carpets and fine furniture. I don't believe this courtesy was to be extended to him in his future days in Alcatraz.

Sammy helped with the camcorder and instruments, and we taped a few darting lights, and few distant sounds, but nothing too startling. The final excitement was to be left to Mike Worden.

Mike decided to explore the length of cellblock 6. He was alone in the dark, taping in infrared inside various cells. Now before I describe the events that followed, Mike asked me to emphasize the fact that in the line of duty as a policeman he has never run from a situation. On the contrary, he unflinchingly goes into potentially dangerous situations and has run down and collared more than his share of suspects. So now that everyone is aware that he is fearless in the world of the living, I can continue the story without tarnishing his reputation, and I will do so from the perspective of his videotape.

Mike is standing in a cell, far down the corridor from the central rotunda. As he is explaining where he is and what he is looking at, there is a loud banging noise that sounds like it is very close to, or actually inside, the small cell in which he is standing. It sounded like a metal pipe striking another metal object. It was loud, it was sharp, and it was very close to Mike.

A second or two later Mike calls out, "Guys, please tell me that was one of you!?"

There is silence. None of our group responds because we aren't anywhere near him. A few seconds more pass and then Mike says, "Okay, maybe it wasn't."

The tension in his voice is obvious. His camcorder is strapped to his belt, and thinking he has stopped recording, he lets the camcorder drop and quickly leaves the cell. However, the camcorder is still running, and recording his feet as they at first begin walking briskly back toward the rotunda. As the tape continues you can see his steps become more rapid. Then he breaks into a full run and his breathing is labored until he finally reaches Bob and Richard at the end of the cellblock.

While I completely understand the terror of the situation—alone in a dark cell with some unknown entity making an unearthly racket right next to you—I couldn't help but laugh myself nearly to tears when I later saw his unique "footage." I wondered if perhaps something did know that Mike was once a prison guard and just wanted to give him a run for his money.

Mike also later explained that in addition to the sound, there was a very strong and frightening presence there as well. It felt threatening and grew so intense that running was the smartest thing he could do. Some people have been critical of the fact that we have all experienced fear at haunted sites. They claim there is nothing to be afraid of and that there's nothing a ghost can do to harm the living. My response to these people is to go right ahead and plunge headfirst into the nastiest haunting they can find, and good luck, because they are going to need it.

By this point we were all painfully cold. I was also quite tired as I was just getting over a head cold, and suggested we head back to the main office across the street from the prison to warm up and take a breather. As I have said in the past, investigations take a lot of mental and emotional energy— there is anticipation, preparation and a heightened state of alertness that is required. Then there is also the physical aspect of being on your feet for hours, lugging around heavy equipment bags and driving long distances. If it is numbingly cold on top of it all, you are going to be one beat little ghost hunter at the end of the night.

It was a great relief when Brian unlocked the prison door and we left the damp, moldy, stale air of the decaying penitentiary. As we entered the warm, lighted office across the street, I had the urge to click together the heels of my hiking boots and declare that there was no place like home—or more accurately, there was nothing like being released from prison.

After sitting for a while drinking hot tea and coffee, we took a consensus on what to do next. Richard and Sammy still had the energy to do more investigating. However, the rest of us agreed we were cold, tired and hungry (since we had started early and never had a chance for dinner), and as we still had a long drive home, we decided to pack up our meters and call it a night. Brian did take Richard and Sammy to a couple of other locations in the prison after we left, but they, too, soon decided to head for home.

In the days that followed we had a lot of videotape and photos to review. I was able to confirm the strange sounds we heard and all the inexplicable white lights moving in the darkness. However, regardless of what physical evidence we obtained, the most compelling evidence that spirits dwell within the massive stone walls of Eastern State Penitentiary comes from the powerful feelings that flood over you.

Looks can be deceiving as you enter the desolate blackness of the abandoned prison. You can feel that you are not alone when you sit in a cell on death row where violent criminals spent their last desperate hours on earth. When motion detectors pierce the silence of an empty corridor, you know it is not your imagination that has triggered the alarms. As you stand shivering in the icy cold of a deserted hospital ward, it is not a coincidence that when your thoughts turn to the pain and suffering that took place inside those walls, something unseen creates a crashing sound behind you.

There may be a dozen tormented spirits still imprisoned at Eastern State, or there may be hundreds. Some may simply be wandering the corridors and courtyards finally seeking a way out, while others may be crouching in darkened corners, filled with the rage and thirst for blood they had in life, waiting for another innocent victim to come to them.

If you have the courage to enter the strong iron gates of the empty penitentiary, don't assume you will be alone, and don't assume you will be safe. Many generations of murderers, rapists and gangsters, who never had any regard for human life, once lived and died there, and it is doubtful that death has changed their evil intent. It is ironic that an institution designed to isolate these criminals to protect society may now be one of the most dangerous places on earth—because now that they are dead, no bars can protect you.

The view from a guard tower of the rooftops of the
crowded cellblocks which radiate from the central rotunda.

Music and Vinyl

In the fall of 2000, I received a call from Tanya Cowen of Jeffersonville, in Sullivan County, New York. She had seen an article in the newspaper about my ghost investigations, and wondered if I would like to check out her music studio, which was in a house on Route 52, where there were apparently several ghosts producing all kinds of phenomena. For example, she said one of her students had seen the man who built the house, which given the fact that he died in the 1960s, made me optimistic that this place would make for a very interesting story.

When my schedule opened up in early 2001, I tried to call Tanya to set up a time for an investigation. However, every time I called I got the answering machine for some church organization, and directory assistance never heard of Tanya or her music studio. While I was disappointed, I assumed she had had enough of her "house guests" and had moved away.

In the fall of 2001, I received another call from a woman who said a friend had seen something about me in the newspaper around Halloween. She said she had a haunted house in Jeffersonville and would like for someone to do an investigation. Before she could continue I asked, "Is this Tanya?" There was a moment's hesitation, as she probably wondered if I was incredibly psychic, and then realized that I was the one she had spoken to a year earlier. I explained that I had been unable to contact her, and before I lost track of her again, I got directions and set up a date for early January.

Bob Strong and I arrived at her house on a chilly Saturday afternoon. It's an attractive, well-kept house in town, facing east toward a stream across the street. There's a garage set back on the right and a backyard bordered by woods. All things considered, it didn't look the least bit spooky.

After Tanya gave us a brief tour, we settled in the living room in the back of the house and I turned on the tape recorder and took notes for the next 45 minutes. The following story emerged:

Tanya bought the house in April of 1998, with the intention of using it as both a place to live, and as a music studio where she would teach piano and flute. While the house was built in the 1940s, the seller was a woman who had lived there with her son for only three years. The woman made no mention of anything unusual happening there, and Tanya had no idea she was getting more than she bargained for. However, the house was to reveal its true nature on moving day.

"The closing was on Good Friday and I started moving in that afternoon," Tanya recalled. "Right away I felt very uncomfortable, as if I wasn't alone. I had been living in an older house just up the road and never felt uncomfortable there." For the most part, Tanya lived in the other house and only used this place for lessons, and was more than happy to leave around 8:30pm every night. However, the place became so unnerving that as she turned out the lights and locked up every night, she would be on the phone talking to her mother or a friend so she wouldn't feel as if she was all alone.

Tanya (left) and her mother, Janice, in front of the house.

Another ongoing problem was that of doors opening on their own. Although everything would be securely closed, doors would be later found standing wide open. Feeling somewhat paranoid about the door situation, Tanya installed latches and locks on every door in the house. While this solved the problem, it created another. Just about every day, she and her students would hear doors rattling and banging, as if someone was angrily trying to open the locked doors.

(At this point I interjected that I feel you should be able to spend the night in a house before you buy it. A lot of misery and grief would be spared by this practice!)

Tanya then continued to say that there would be cold spots and icy breezes with no logical explanation. The staircase leading from the front parlor (which she converted to the piano lesson room) to the upstairs attic space frequently was the site of strange noises. Both Tanya and her students always felt as if someone was watching them from those stairs (which was to their backs as they played the piano) and many times they would turn quickly around, fully expecting to see someone standing there. Tanya said the feeling was so strong her hair would stand on end and it was difficult to sit with her back to that staircase for any length of time, and nearly impossible to actually sit on the stairs.

Wanting some answers, Tanya and her family discovered that the house was built by a man named Vinyl Philips. He lived in the house until the 1960s, when he died suddenly of an aneurysm in his brain—while sitting in the front parlor. He had outlived two wives, one of whom had Tourette's syndrome. In addition to doing the actual construction of the place, he loved to tinker on many projects, and was clearly attached to the home he had made. It was rapidly becoming obvious to Tanya that Vinyl, and perhaps one or both of his wives, had never really moved out.

The first tangible event occurred in January of 1999. Tanya entered the house with two young female students and left them for a minute to get some things ready. When she came back in the front parlor, she heard the sound of water running. Entering the bathroom in the back right of the house, she found that the hot water was streaming out of the faucet at full force. She assumed one of the girls had turned it on for some reason, yet the mirror over the sink was already steamed over, which would have taken more than a minute or two.

Nevertheless, there was no other rational explanation, so Tanya reprimanded the two girls for what she thought was a silly prank. Both girls appeared to have no idea what she was talking about, and said they hadn't even left the piano room, let alone gone down the hall, turned on the hot water and returned without Tanya noticing them.

Lights began to flicker, and several checks of the wiring produced no explanations. There was also the distinct sound of the chain of a light switch being clicked on, but no one else would be in the house at the time, and no lights would actually go on. (This would be a phenomenon I would experience firsthand, and record on videotape.)

Then in the spring of 1999, came the most disturbing evidence of a haunting. Around 3:30pm one afternoon there was a steady and persistent banging noise coming from the basement. In sounded like hammering, but not with a metal hammer. It had the dull thudding sound of a wooden mallet pounding against wood, and it sounded as though it was directly under the back living room in the basement. It continued until about 5pm when it stopped as mysteriously as it began.

The next day the pounding began again about 3:30pm, and once again lasted until about 5pm. The pipes were all checked and nothing could be found to explain the noise. This continued day after day, the sound rising up from under the floor of the back room, right from the area where Vinyl Philip's workbench still stood!

Tanya was not the only one to hear the hammering—her mother, Janice, was sitting in the back room while Tanya was giving a young boy a piano lesson in the front parlor. After the boy left, Janice asked Tanya, "Why did you let that boy keep pounding the pedals of the piano like that?" Tanya explained that the boy was actually so small his feet couldn't even reach the pedals. What they believe her mother had heard was Vinyl Philips hammering at his workbench.

On another occasion, Tanya was giving a mother and daughter a piano lesson while another younger daughter was in the back room watching a video. After the lesson the little girl complained that she kept hearing a banging noise and the room was icy cold. It was a hot July afternoon, and there wasn't any air conditioning, and there was no one else in the house. On another hot summer's day, a woman waiting for her daughter had to go out to her car and get a blanket in order to be able to withstand the bizarre cold of that room.

The hammering sound continued day after day at the same time until it was decided to take a drastic step—Tanya's father dragged the old workbench out of the basement and threw it away. From that day the hammering stopped.

However, the area may still contain Vinyl's energy. Tanya told a friend, Tony Macaluso, about all of the strange occurrences. Tony is a retired New York City policeman and is not only fascinated by the "theory of spirits not at rest," he also has always known he "had a sixth sense" about places and things that had yet to happen. Although he didn't know where in the basement the workbench had been, as soon as he went down the stairs he pointed to the right and told Tanya that was the spot where Vinyl had worked. Tony said he felt a distinct tingling sensation that had immediately directed him to that spot. (He was to feel that tingling sensation in another curious spot in the basement—but more on that later.)

What had been the nature of this phantom building project? Remarkably, a three-year mystery was to be solved the very afternoon that I was conducting the investigation. While I was there, Tanya telephoned her grandmother to get some details about the people who lived in the area. During the conversation, her grandmother said, "By the way, I got a Christmas card from Vinyl's daughter. She happened to mention that her father built a boat down in the basement one winter. He cut and fit all the pieces together, then in the spring took it apart and put it back together outside."

A boat builder would not use a metal hammer and nails. He would use a wooden mallet to pound the wooden pieces into place. Apparently, it was not uncommon to build a boat indoors in the cold weather, and then since it would be too large to fit up the stairs or out the door, to disassemble the boat into manageable sections and reassemble it outdoors when the weather got warm. And, where else would Vinyl work on his project but by his workbench?

While I really never believe anything is a coincidence, even this information surprised me. Within an hour of hearing the story about the mysterious pounding sounds of wood striking wood by Vinyl's workbench every afternoon, I hear that he built a boat there! Now that's my idea of cooperation from the other side.

Unfortunately, the removal of the workbench did not end the strange happenings. One afternoon while Tanya was out, she had her piano tuned. When she came home later, the two men commented that as they worked an awful lot of people had come into the house and left again, which they assumed was accomplished through a side or back entrance. They didn't actually see anyone, but they heard many footsteps on the floor above them.

When they found out that no one else could have possibly entered the house, because the only unlocked door was the front door right by the piano, they both gasped and exclaimed, "Oh, my god!" To put it mildly, Tanya said they were both "freaked out."

One evening as Tanya gave a lesson to a young girl, they both heard a terrible racket upstairs. Tanya was convinced someone had broken in, and hurried the girl into another room, locked the door and called her father, who lived close by. He was there in minutes, and as he entered the house he also heard the banging and crashing sounds upstairs. Rushing upstairs to confront the intruder, he found no one, and absolutely nothing out of place. They checked all the doors, windows and closets, and found that everything was secure and undisturbed.

As startling as this was, the most dramatic occurrence was to happen in June of 1999. Tanya and a student (a girl of about sixteen who was unaware of any stories about the place being haunted) were in the flute room, which is directly off the piano room in the front of the house. There is a doorway from the flute room leading to the kitchen, so if you are seated in the right position, you can see the kitchen, hallway and piano room. In the middle of the lesson, the girl suddenly gasped, her eyes grew wide and she looked very pale. In fact, Tanya said she looked "as white as a ghost." They were appropriate words to choose, because the girl had just seen an apparition as plain and distinct as any living being, with a few slight differences—which are understandable when one has been dead for thirty years.

When Tanya asked what was the matter, the girl began to whisper, "I just saw a man. He walked from the hallway into the piano room!" Tanya immediately checked the piano room, and the hallway, and the kitchen and the rest of the rooms, but no other living being was in that house.

31

The girl described the figure as an older man of average build, wearing glasses and a plaid shirt. His overall appearance was very gray in color. His most remarkable feature was actually a lack of a particular feature—namely legs. From the waist down the man was somewhat misty and faded. He didn't so much as walk as he "moved" through the hall and into the piano room. From the moment of his appearance, the entire house was icy cold the rest of the day.

Tanya finally realized that she now had no hope of trying to explain away everything else that had happened.

"I knew that they were telling me, 'We are here. This is our house!' Of course I wasn't happy about it, but since it seemed as though they were here to stay, I said, 'Okay, you're here, but I don't ever want to see you!' And so far, they haven't appeared to me. I guess they just don't know that they are dead. They wonder what I'm doing here with my music and students."

Although Tanya has never witnessed an apparition (in human form, at least) she has heard disembodied voices on many occasions. Often, when she first arrives in the morning, as she is opening the front door she hears a man's and woman's voice in the kitchen—it is just as if a couple is having a pleasant conversation at breakfast. Janice Cowen has also heard conversations coming from the kitchen, which abruptly stop when she goes to investigate.

There have also been strange outbursts of words from out of thin air. While Tanya and a student sat at the piano, a loud female voice blurted out, "Hello!" right behind them.

"We both froze. Then we looked at each other and my student asked if I had heard that. I told her to tell me first what she heard. She did hear the "Hello," and we both agreed it sounded like it came from someone who had no control over her voice."

There were to be many such inexplicable outbursts of words from this phantom female. As Tanya tried to make sense of this bizarre phenomena, she learned that one of Vinyl's wives suffered from Tourette's Syndrome—a disease in which one of the symptoms is sudden swearing or uncontrollable verbal outbursts. Perhaps this affliction has followed Vinyl's wife even into death?

Another voice spoke to Tanya in the fall of 2001. As she was walking up the basement stairs, there was a loud, startling banging noise right behind her. She whipped around, but saw that nothing had fallen, and there wasn't anything visible that could have caused the noise. Then suddenly a male voice said loud and clear, "Sorry!" That was all her nerves could stand and she slammed the basement door and securely locked it.

There were also some instances that seemed to be acts of mischief. When her cousin came for a lesson, she removed her retainer and placed it in her instrument case. The next day, her cousin called to say she couldn't find her retainer. Tanya saw her put it in the case, but searched the house from top to bottom anyway, with no luck. Then three days later she walked into one of the rooms and there in plain sight was the retainer on a table! There wasn't anything else on the table, and the retainer could not have been overlooked there for three days—especially since she was specifically searching for it.

This hide and seek game continued one day with the key to the garage. Tanya and her mother searched high and low and finally decided it was lost forever. Then one day her mother was by the sink in the kitchen and she heard a clinking sound just a foot or two away. Looking over to the countertop, there lay the garage key! It was in the middle of the counter, with nothing else around it, as if someone had just dropped it there.

Similar things were to occur with Tanya's checkbook and other items, and each time, after extensive searches, the items would show up in plain site on a table or the kitchen counter. Although it would be easy to blame Vinyl and his wives for these events, perhaps these weren't actually cases of mischief—perhaps the spirits were actually being helpful by returning things she had really lost. At least Tanya's mother considered this possibility when she told Tanya, "When these things reappear, just say 'Thank you!'"

Then there clearly was some outright mischief. During the Christmas season of 1999, Tanya placed an artificial tree in the corner of the piano room. As part of the decorations, she had put twelve candy canes spread out across the tree. As she was entering the house one morning, she heard a woman's footsteps hurrying across the floor and up the stairs. No one could be found, but when she looked at the Christmas tree, she saw that all twelve candy canes had been placed on the same branch!

Although so much has happened in the four years she has owned the house, there was a definite turning point in both the quantity and the nature of the activity. In May and June of 2000, the house was remodeled. The staircase to the top floor was sealed off, although the ends of the railings and bottom step were left. A new staircase was built in the back living room and the upstairs was finished in a beautiful natural wood. After these changes were made, the number of strange events decreased significantly, and for the most part, Tanya asserts that what did still happen was not as negative. The renovations seemed to shift the paranormal energy from that of resentment and antagonism, to something more benign, or even what could be considered friendly.

For example, one evening Tanya reached up to pull the chain on a ceiling lamp to turn it on, when something suddenly yanked her arm back. At that moment, the large glass globe on the fixture fell off and smashed on the floor. Had her arm not been pulled out of the way by a mysterious force, the glass would have shattered on her hand.

There was also the time she came home from shopping and had bags in both hands. As she came up the front steps one of her sneakers got caught and she began falling forward. Since her hands were full, she was unable to bring her arms up fast enough to break her fall, and she was heading face first into a pillar.

"I was sure I was going to have all of my teeth knocked out," Tanya recalled. "But something stopped me. One instant my body was falling forward and my face was about to hit the pillar, and the next I was standing straight up! There was no way I could have done that myself."

However, even some non-threatening phenomena can be terrifying. About a year after the remodeling was complete, Tanya was in the upstairs bedroom talking on the phone to a friend. It was about 10:30pm, and she noticed her cat was acting agitated and began staring at something in the direction of the closet. Tanya looked to where the cat was looking, and there in front of the closet was a white mist. It didn't have any particular shape, it was just a cloud-like mass hovering in the air.

She described to her friend what she was seeing, and her friend replied that she was hanging up, because she was so terrified that she feared whatever the mist was could somehow affect her over the phone! Tanya sat alone and scared, and watched as the mist simply faded and disappeared after a few minutes. Nothing like that had ever happened before, and fortunately for Tanya, it never did again.

Just a week before I arrived, another strange thing happened involving the upstairs. Tanya has one of those large exercise balls—which for the past year was collecting dust in a corner near the bed. She hadn't moved it in all that time, and even with windows open and breezes blowing in, the ball remained undisturbed in its place. Then one evening as she went to go upstairs, she saw that the ball was sitting on the top of stairs, as if poised to come bouncing down the steps. There was simply no logical explanation as to why that ball should left the corner, traveled over twenty feet and perched itself at the top of the stairs.

Of course, the inexplicable is routine in this Jeffersonville house. A videotape once flew across the room. Tanya's dogs growl at thin air, vertical blinds move as if someone has just walked through them, and terrible crashing sounds occur throughout the house, although nothing is ever out of place.

After experiencing a convincing number of bizarre events, Tanya finally found the courage to ask the former owner if she or her son had ever seen a ghost, or at least felt or heard anything unusual. The woman did admit that they frequently heard strange noises. She also said that she once took a photo of her son in the house, and in the picture there appeared to be a man's face and eyes. Some guests were upstairs and swore that they saw faces looking in

The exercise ball sits in the corner where it had for a year, until it came across the floor on its own to the top of the staircase.

through the windows at them (which would be physically impossible without a tall ladder).

There was also an electrical problem. Every time she tried to plug in something in the corner of the parlor the fuse would blow—until she put a reading lamp there. It seems that Vinyl used to sit in that corner and read every evening, so she tried to accommodate him by giving him a light. For whatever the reason, the fuses never again blew after that.

Tanya also discovered that in the 1970s, the man who lived in the house claimed that the place was haunted and used to tell everyone in town about the ghosts. However, as the man was known to be suffering from mental illness no one ever took him seriously. It now appears while he might have been ill, he probably wasn't crazy after all!

Of course, it would have been nice to know all of this before buying the house, but even so, the

The lamp for Vinyl.

information was helpful in dealing with the situation. Although confirming that your house has been haunted for decades is not exactly comforting news, it is always good to know that you are not hallucinating or losing your mind.

After recording all of these fascinating stories, it was time to break out our equipment and see what science had to say about it. Our first stop was a tiny storage room/closet in the basement, which ironically has a large sign above it reading, "SPIRITS." Although they assume the sign simply indicates that it was once used to store liquor, both Tanya and her mother refuse to go near it, and Tony felt that strange tingling there, too. While most people utilize every square inch of storage space in their homes, the shelves in this closet remain empty. Even with all that has occurred, this is the only place in the house where Tanya is truly scared to go.

We decided to set up the infrared camcorder there first. As I was getting it ready, I looked through the viewfinder and could already see those small white spots zipping around. Also, in order to rule out any dust or particles that we may have stirred up, we left the camcorder running and went back upstairs to give the air time to settle down. However, long after we were gone, these strange lights continued to move in front of this mysterious SPIRITS closet.

The "Spirits" sign over the closet in the basement.

Bob later took some digital photos in the basement, and those strange orbs showed up in two places. There were many in the oil tank room, although no particular paranormal activity had previously been connected to that room. The other area where a few orbs appeared was right where Vinyl's workbench once stood. This area also had some high EMF readings, and there were no electrical lines or appliances in the area to explain the readings. The area is essentially bare concrete and cinder blocks—substances that do not create electromagnetic fields.

The only other place in the house where we photographed orbs was right on the walled-up old staircase. Prior to its removal during the renovations in

2000, this was an area of almost constant inexplicable sounds and unnerving feelings. While the physical stairs are gone, the energy of the place may remain.

Two orbs appeared on and near the walled-up staircase.

While everyone remained in the back living room to minimize noise and disturbances, I walked through the dark house by myself, taping in infrared. Nothing much happened, until I entered the piano room (which was Vinyl's parlor). As I was walking toward the spot where Vinyl used to sit and read, I heard the distinctive clinking sound of a pull chain switch of a lamp that Tanya had said she had heard on several occasions. I immediately turned toward the ceiling light in the center of the room over the piano, but the chains hung motionless, and, of course, the light didn't go on.

I waited for about 30 seconds, but nothing else happened. However, just as I turned the camcorder away the clinking sound occurred again—loud and clear, and just a few feet above me (both sounds were recorded by the camcorder). Again I turned the camcorder toward the light, but nothing moved and the sound did not occur again. I got the distinct impression I was being played with, and while I appreciate the opportunity to record such sounds, I never like being the subject of a prank. As much as I was tempted to give them a piece of my mind, I thought it best to keep my mouth shut and let them have their fun. It's never wise to antagonize the dead.

Since the piano room was obviously one of the centers of activity, if not *the* center, I set up the camcorder on the tripod, aimed it toward the corner were Vinyl used to sit, and left the room and closed the door. I didn't view that footage until we got home, and was literally startled at what I heard.

For several minutes nothing happened—no white spots zipping around, no strange sounds, no movement. There were only the sounds of passing cars and the ticking of a pendulum clock that hung on the wall to the left of the camera. I sat on the floor in front of our 36" television carefully looking and listening for anything unusual. Suddenly, I realized the ticking of the clock seemed irregular. At first the ticking was clear and distinct, but then the ticking sound began to fade. I increased the volume and crept closer and closer to the television, turning my head toward the speakers to try to hear the fading sounds of the clock.

Just as the volume was way up, and the sounds of the ticking seemed to cease completely, there was a loud "BANG!" The sudden, sharp metallic banging sound caught me completely off guard and sent me reeling backward onto my rear end. My initial reaction was, "Damn it, he got me again!"

Sitting back a little further, I turned down the volume and continued watching. Within a minute there was another banging sound, even louder than the first. It was like two large, heavy pieces of metal crashing together. This time I was more prepared for the sound and was mildly pleased that he didn't get me twice. (When you do enough ghost investigations you really do start thinking like this!)

After the two banging noises, there was silence, except for the ticking of the clock, which gained in strength and was again loud and clear. As soon as I finished reviewing the tape, I e-mailed Tanya to ask if any of her pipes or radiators made loud banging noises, and she replied that they never had in the four years she lived there. I sent her a copy of the tape, and she confirmed that those noises in the piano room were unlike anything she had ever heard.

Even though we did not photograph any spirits wearing plaid shirts, or record footsteps or conversations, I would say this was still a rather successful ghost investigation. While it appears that Vinyl and his wives (and perhaps others yet to be identified) still reside in the home he built, they seem to be reconciled that Tanya and her music students are there to stay. And although you may not have the opportunity to meet the spirits of these people, you can visit the cemetery where their bodies are buried. If you are traveling west on Route 17B, they are buried in the large cemetery right before you come to White Lake.

If you do visit their graves, you may want to say a pray and remind them that it is time to move on. Perhaps they will finally trade the piano room for some place that has harps.

A few orbs appeared in the oil tank room in the basement.

Trolley View Farm

After presenting a ghost lecture at the Goshen Library in October of 2001, a local couple asked me if I might be interested in investigating their house. In fact, it might be the oldest house in Goshen, New York, believed to have been built around 1740. There was a major addition in 1830, and it became the center of a large, successful farm. The owners, Joe and Kathy, told me just enough to pique my curiosity, so early in 2002, on a cold clear night illuminated by a full moon, Bob and I went to see for ourselves what was happening in the old farmhouse.

The farm received its name because a trolley
once ran directly in front of the house.

Joe's family bought the house in 1965 and his father was the first to encounter something strange. It was late at night and the family was asleep on the second floor, when his father was awakened by loud noises. After getting out of bed, he clearly heard the creaking of the outside metal cellar doors as they were opened and then slammed shut. This was followed by footsteps and the sounds of something being dragged or scraped—almost like a lame man dragging his leg across the floor. There was also heavy, labored breathing, indicating some great effort was being expended. Then the intruder walked and dragged his way up the cellar steps, and clicked on the light switch, as if preparing to open the door and enter the first floor.

That was enough. In the darkness, his father found the telephone, felt for the "zero" and dialed the operator.

"Please send the police! Someone has broken into my house," he whispered to the operator.

Within minutes the police arrived. They searched the house from top to bottom and didn't find anyone. There also wasn't any evidence of a break-in, and no discernable way for someone to have gained entry to the locked house. The police said it just must have been typical old house sounds—but since when are opening doors, footsteps, dragging sounds and a light switch turning on typical?

The three children weren't told anything about the episode, but they didn't need to hear about what had happened to their father to be frightened—enough would happen to them. One day when Joe was in the bathroom, his younger brother hid in an adjacent room with plans of jumping out to scare him. Before the plot could be sprung, Joe suddenly opened the bathroom door and yelled, "What? Why are you calling me?"

His brother sheepishly came out of his hiding place and said he didn't want anything.

'Then why were you calling me?" Joe replied, exasperated, and then slammed the door closed.

It wasn't until many years later that his brother finally told Joe that he hadn't made a sound, and that he hadn't heard any voice that day. Joe was incredulous, because he had distinctly heard a male voice calling his name.

There would be a similar occurrence thirty years later. Joe and his wife Kathy had bought the house from his parents, and while he was outside fixing a window, she was busy inside doing laundry and housework. All of a sudden she came out of the door in a somewhat agitated state and said, "What! What do you want?"

"What do you mean, what do I want?" Joe replied completely puzzled.

"Why do you keep calling me if you don't want anything?" Kathy said, adamant about the fact that a male voice had repeatedly yelled, "Kathy."

Joe assured her that he hadn't said a word, and it became evident that someone, or something, was up to its old tricks.

Unfortunately, not all of the inexplicable events of Joe's childhood were so harmless. In fact, some were so traumatic he still has difficulty talking about them today. When he was about seven, he and his brother were asleep in the bedroom they shared. All of a sudden he awoke, and found that the room was bathed in light. Afraid to move, he turned his eyes toward the window, and to his horror saw the figure of a man standing outside the window. This was a second-story window with no ledge or roof beneath it. But that wasn't the only problem.

The man was glowing brightly. Even his hair and beard were glowing. The man, visible from the waist up, stared straight ahead through the window toward the closet on the opposite wall. Joe was terrified of making a sound or movement, because he didn't want this man to know he was there. Minutes passed, the glowing man remained staring through the window, and Joe couldn't stand it anymore. He began screaming for his mother.

It was only a few moments before she entered the room, but in that time both the light and the man disappeared. She tried to explain to her distraught son that it was only a dream, or lights from the highway. He may have only been seven, but he knew that he had been awake, and he told her it was definitely the ghost of a bearded man that had been at his window.

As if the glowing man hadn't been bad enough, the next night would be even worse. He awoke again in the middle of the night with the feeling that someone else was in the room. Daring to look at the window, he was relieved to find that no one was there. Unfortunately, his relief was short-lived, for as he turned over toward his brother's bed by the closet, he glimpsed something on the floor, between the beds. Inching cautiously forward, he peered over the edge of the bed a saw a hand.

The hand was that of a grown man, and it slowly swung out from under his bed until it was visible almost up to the elbow, and then slowly swung back under the bed. The fingers slowly moved in a motion similar to that of strumming a tabletop. And the reason Joe was able to see this hand and arm in the dark was because it, too, was giving off a light of its own—softly glowing a pale green color.

Once again Joe was frozen with fear. This time, however, the terror gripped him even tighter, because it was no longer a case of something being outside his window—whatever this was, it was right underneath him! Watching with mesmerizing horror, the arm continued the same slow motion back and forth, back and forth under the bed. Joe's face was so close to the arm he was able to see the size and shape of the fingernails, and the hair on the arm.

Joe finally ended the silent terror by screaming at the top of his lungs. His father came running in to find out what was the matter. Joe explained that a glowing hand was under his bed.

"There aren't any monsters under your bed!" his father said angrily.

"It's not a monster, it's a ghost!" Joe insisted, and then refused to go back to sleep in that bed.

"All right, then get in your brother's bed, but just go back to sleep," his father said, clearly not happy with what he considered to be childish hysterics.

Joe's brother was none too happy, either. He was terrified by his brother's description of the hand, and as the two boys huddled in the one bed, his brother finally asked what they had both been thinking.

"Do you think it's still there?"

Joe hesitated to look, but he had to know. Slowly turning his head toward his empty bed, he gasped when he saw that the hand had returned. He begged and pleaded with his brother to look, but the terrified boy refused. Joe had no alternative but to start screaming again.

"Okay, that's it!" his father shouted, storming into the room. Grabbing the end of Joe's bed, he lifted it into the air. "Look, there's nothing under here. Now go to sleep!"

This time both boys refused to get into either bed, so their father made them sit against the wall out in the hall so they could think about how foolish they were being. After their father went back to bed, Joe's brother once again asked, "Do you think it's still there?" Joe leaned over and peered around the doorway, and to his great relief the hand had not returned. After sitting for quite a while in the hall, they became drowsy and finally both got into his brother's bed and went to sleep. Joe would not return to his own bed for several months, and to this day he still asks his brother, "Why couldn't you have just looked?"

In some fascinating twists to this episode, despite his father's anger and insistence that there was nothing there, many years later he admitted to Joe that he had also once had a similar experience with a hand coming out from under his bed! And while doing some research on the house, Joe found out that around the 1930s, a farmhand named Ebb was trying to steal money and jewelry from the house, but was apprehended when he was found hiding underneath one of the beds. Ebb was to spend eight years in Sing Sing prison for the crime, and although it may have nothing to do with the glowing hand, it's interesting to note.

Things were then relatively quiet until Joe reached his teens. His bedroom was moved to the first floor in what they refer to as the back room, although it is actually the first room on your left when you enter the front door (which is rarely used now). Several times Joe would be awakened by a strong force pushing him down, like the pressure of being underwater. This feeling would also be experienced by Kathy's father many years later when he stayed in the second floor bedroom in the oldest part of the house.

Due to his many strange experiences, Joe searched for answers, although probably not in the wisest way. One day he announced that if any spirits wanted to communicate or enter this world, he would act as a conduit for them. As I have also learned the hard way, be careful what you ask for!

Many bizarre things then began to happen in that back room. Perhaps the most dramatic took place during the day, when he was on his bed. He glanced over to the corner across the room, and there stood the dark outline of a young boy, perhaps four feet tall. Before Joe had time to react, the small figure charged across the room and appeared to jump on top of him. Joe started swinging his fists, but they passed through the boy's head and hit the bed. When he finally caught onto something relatively solid, the boy simply vanished. Joe eventually decided to retract his open invitation to the other world.

After living at different locations for several years, Joe returned to the house with his wife in 1993. Joe's parents lived with them for a short time, and nothing unusual happened until the week after his parents moved out. Joe often worked the late night shift, while Kathy had left her job on Wall Street to work locally, so she would have more time to raise the first of their three daughters. In the morning she would get ready for work, feed the baby and get her dressed, and arrive at work around 9am.

One morning, she was upstairs getting the baby ready when she heard something downstairs. First, there was a loud and distinct sound of something being dragged or scraped along the floor (not unlike Joe's father's experience back in 1965). Then it sounded like the door of the woodstove was creaking back and forth. Assuming it had to be their cat rubbing up against the woodstove, she ignored it. When the sounds grew louder, as if heavy equipment was being moved around, she couldn't imagine how the cat was able to make such a racket, and she started feeling a bit anxious.

Kathy yelled for the cat to cut it out, but no sooner had the words left her lips when she saw that the cat was curled up on the floor, and had obviously been there for some time. Realizing that this was no natural disturbance, she picked up her daughter, said, "Come on, we're going to work early today," and rushed out of the house without daring to search for whatever had been making all the noise.

However, things that are silent can just as easily catch your attention. For instance, there is the recurring apparition of the "Dark Man." He appears to either be the spirit of a black man, or is just a very dark, shadowy form, about six feet tall. The Dark Man has been seen numerous times in the living room. Kathy has also seen him in their bedroom. One time he moved out of the corner and approached the bed before he vanished. The next morning she found that one of her bras had been taken out of a drawer and placed on top of the dresser.

Their three daughters have not been told about the sightings of the Dark Man, but one night Joe felt that something strange was going on—that something was in the house. The following morning all of the girls said they had had nightmares. When asked what they had dreamed about, they all described a dark man.

Is there any possible explanation to link a dark man to the old farmhouse? Ebb, the man caught under the bed with the jewelry had been black, as were many of the farmhands. In fact, Ebb's brother, Fritz, met a very tragic end not too far from the house. It had been reported that Fritz was a bit too fond of liquor. One night he was particularly drunk and took off with his dog, Butch. The next day, Fritz and Butch were both found decapitated on the railroad tracks. The police speculated that Fritz was so drunk he passed out on the tracks, and his ever-faithful dog Butch stayed by his side, even though a train was bearing down on them.

Of course, this was only speculation, and no one could say for sure that foul play wasn't involved. As faithful and protective as dogs are, it is difficult to believe that a dog would allow himself to be run over by a train. Is it possible then, that Fritz and his dog had been murdered, and then placed on the tracks to make it look like an accident? This too, is only speculation, but worth considering. And, as Joe has sometimes felt something like a dog brush or push against his leg, perhaps both Fritz and Butch keep returning to the farmhouse to remind the world of the living about their tragic deaths.

On the other end of the apparition spectrum is the Lady in White. She first appeared to Kathy in the bedroom. The woman stood silently at the foot of the bed long enough for Kathy to give a detailed description. She looked very much like one of the famous Gibson Girls—upswept hair, high-collared white blouse with puffed sleeves, a belt around the waist and a long skirt. The only feature that wasn't distinct was the woman's face. The hair and neck were very clear, but for some reason she would not reveal her identity. Moments after the woman disappeared, an icy cold wind passed across Kathy's face. (It is interesting to note that the Dark Man made one of his appearances in the bedroom the very next night.)

The next time the Lady in White was seen, it was about 3am and Joe was stripping wallpaper from the hallway that passes between the front and back doors. Using a steamer and a scraper, he was slowly removing five layers of paper, which no doubt represented many years of history of the old house. As he worked, he saw a figure moving to his left, near the back door. The woman in white—with upswept hair, a high-collared blouse and long skirt—walked past the door and into the living room.

Joe called out, asking who was there and received no response. Hardly believing what he had just seen, he entered the living room and switched on the light. No one was there, and there wasn't any other way out of the room.

There has also been a third witness in recent times. Joe's friend, Paul, had been visiting one night, and as he was leaving he suddenly hesitated by the back door. He turned around and looked at Joe with an odd expression.

"I think I just saw your ghost!" Paul said with all seriousness.

He went on to explain that as he reached for the doorknob, a woman's reflection appeared in the glass of the door. She was wearing a white blouse, and appeared to be dressed in an old fashioned style. She also appeared to be standing in the same spot in the hallway where Joe had first seen her.

The hallway where Joe and Paul both saw the Lady in White. One of our photos revealed an orb (see arrow) right where Joe was stripping wallpaper when he saw the woman walk by.

Joe and Kathy came to believe that this Lady in White was the spirit of a woman who lived in the house for over ninety years and died around 1960. However, after recently speaking to the woman's great-grandson, they may have to rethink that theory. When Joe asked the man if there were any ghost stories connected with his old family home, the man replied that there were rumors about "a woman who haunted the house." Since these stories existed when his great-grandmother was still alive, at least one female ghost pre-dates her.

Perhaps connected with the Lady in White is the flowery scent that Kathy has detected numerous times in that same hallway, or on the staircase above. Like roses or perfume, the scent can be very strong and distinct, yet Joe has been unable to smell it, even though he and Kathy would be standing side by side at the time the aroma was present. Kathy has also smelled pipe tobacco smoke, which Joe is unable to detect.

Another common, yet unusual, phenomenon occurs with the lamps in the living room. They turn on by themselves. This tends to happen more frequently when other strange things have happened, or if something is about to happen. I asked when was the last time this occurred, and found out the lights came on by themselves just a few hours before we arrived. Joe then admitted, "I asked everyone to put on a good show for you tonight." The lights were on, the spiritual invitations were sent out and we were about to walk right into the middle of the show.

After I finished taking notes, there was still too much light to start the infrared camcorder, so as Bob took some photos, I took some readings with the EMF meter. Nothing seemed out of the ordinary in the living room, until I came to the window that looked out into the courtyard area in the backyard. There was a strong electromagnetic field there, and the hair stood up on the back of my neck. I checked for electrical outlets or anything that might be causing the high readings, but it seemed to be only right by the glass of the window. I had the very strong feeling that a man was standing right outside looking in. Then I noticed a mylar balloon (which had been for Kathy's mother's birthday) to my right that started moving rapidly back and forth. The show had apparently already begun!

Having little hope of any meaningful answer, I nonetheless asked if there might be any reason for feeling as if there was a man looking at me just inches away on

Bob took this photo of me taking notes, just minutes before I discovered the high EMF readings by this window, saw the balloon swinging back and forth and felt a strong male presence. The balloon is directly behind me, standing still. If any breezes had been present, they should have made the balloon move earlier.

47

the other side of the thin panes of glass. Kathy surprised me by saying that when her father visited he would stand by that window for long periods of time, just gazing out. When he wanted to smoke a cigarette, he would go outside and stand right next to this same window, staring in.

He had passed away just eight weeks earlier, and she had felt his presence in the house several times since then. In fact, the night he died, Joe told Kathy he heard a strange moaning sound between 2am and 3am, and was afraid her father had passed away. (I should make it clear her father was *not* staying with them at the time, and there was no immediate concern for his health.) They got the call the next morning that he had died unexpectedly during the night, possibly just at the time Joe heard the strange moaning.

Perhaps her father was standing there at that very moment, making his presence known, and moving the balloon that had helped celebrate his wife's birthday. All things considered, I didn't doubt it.

As soon as it was dark, we set up the camcorder in the living room. Almost immediately, several small white spots moved toward the camera. (Again, I must give the usual disclaimer that these could be airborne particles.) While we left the camera running on the tripod, we went next to the back room. This was the room that had been Joe's bedroom was he was in his teens. It is now a sitting room and also serves as the place where Joe paints his wonderful early-American style paintings of local scenes.

I scanned the room with the EMF meter and found nothing until I approached the couch. The readings grew steadily higher the closer I got to the couch. Curious to see how far the electromagnetic field extended, I leaned forward and stretched out my arm. Instantly, an electric jolt shot through my hand and up to my shoulder. It was so strong I staggered back several steps and almost dropped the meter. I told Bob to quickly take a picture with the digital camera and within seconds of the jolt he captured an image of a long, serpentine white light over the couch. It was about four or five feet long and stretched from the window to the center of the couch.

Bob immediately took several more photos, and while the streak was gone, there was a pale, round light spot on the wall near where the left end of the streak had appeared. The next few images showed nothing unusual, but a few minutes later he took another picture and on the wall above the couch there was a faint round area and next to it a small patch a few inches long that appeared red and blue. No other photos showed anything strange.

It didn't take long for me to get over the initial shock (although the tingling continued for several minutes), and I once again dared to hold out my arm, but now the meter read zero. I moved around the room and back to the couch area several times, but there were no further positive readings. Whatever it was had gone.

The streak of light that appeared over the couch
just seconds after I received the electric shock.
There is also a bright orb by the piano.

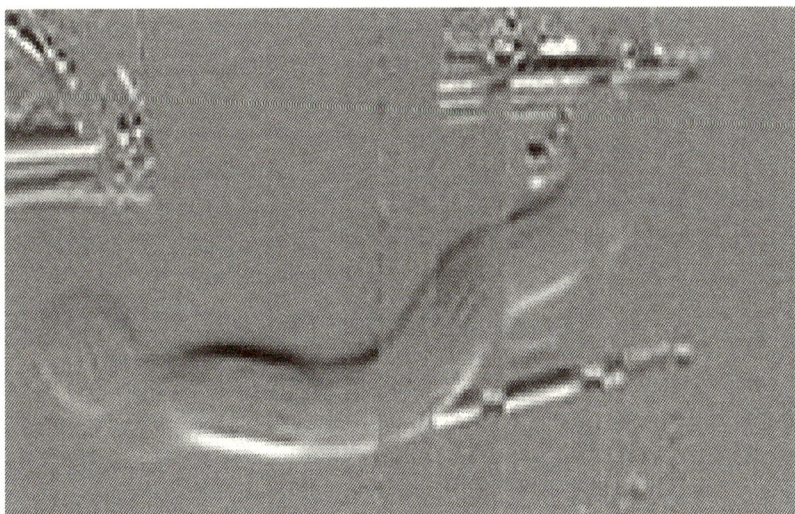

I generally don't computer enhance any photographic images, but since this streak really caught my attention, I tried a few techniques. This was the result of applying embossing to the streak, which made it look three-dimensional. (Or should that be fourth or fifth-dimensional?)

I had never before felt such a jolt, and while I can't say what caused it, I can rule out a couple of things. First, it wasn't like the static electricity shock you feel sliding your feet across a carpet and then touching a piece of metal. I hadn't touched anything, and this was far more powerful than one of those little zaps. It was more akin to the feeling you get when you accidentally try to plug in something while your finger is making contact with one of the prongs. Even so, this was a sharper, more directed jolt, and I had trouble moving my fingers for a couple of minutes.

It also could not have been caused by the meter itself, which only runs on a single 9-volt battery. I have never had any kind of shock from the meter and the wiring is all intact and encased in the hard plastic covering.

As for the streak of light in the photo, we also looked for any natural explanations. There were no lamps or any other light sources in the room near the window or the couch. There are cars that pass by, so we considered that headlights had somehow caused the streak. We tried to duplicate the effect, but car headlights were unable to create even a small spot, let alone a five-foot streak.

Later in the evening, we set up the infrared camcorder in the back room and recorded many strange little white spots moving around the room. These were definitely not specks of dust, as they moved swiftly, changed direction abruptly, and seemed to be most prevalent when Joe was in the room. Joe also experienced what I call the "cobweb effect" there—as if some wispy substance is brushing against your skin. Trying to brush or wipe away whatever it is has no effect, it's almost as if something is under your skin.

Our next stop was upstairs, which has a bizarre story of its own. The original 1740 house was a small structure with only a couple of rooms. The impressive two-story main house addition was built in 1830. The structure was of a beautiful classic design, but during the 1950s the owners did the unthinkable—they removed the grand staircase and the entire second story! They claimed that it cost too much to heat during the winter, which even if that was true, is no excuse to butcher a lovely house. They could have simply closed off the upstairs during the cold months, and still have enjoyed the second floor the rest of the year. It is very tempting to speculate that there were other more unusual and compelling reasons for the radical removal of half the house, but it would only be speculation. Later modifications added back two bedrooms upstairs, with a hallway and a few steps leading down to the upstairs room of the 1740 structure, but it would take major renovations to return the house to its 19th century appearance.

We first went to the Joe and Kathy's bedroom, where the Lady in White and the Dark Man have both been seen. Bob and Kathy were near the door, and Joe and I were on the other side of the room in the corner where the Dark Man has appeared out of the shadows, when that vertigo/disoriented

Trolley View farm as it appeared in the 1940s. This photo was taken for insurance purposes, to show the damage inflicted by a storm. Note the second story, columns and porch.

The Trolley View Farm today, with the second story removed.

feeling hit me. As at the Farnsworth House in Gettysburg, I looked down to see if the floorboards were bending, and moved my feet back and forth to try to keep my balance. I didn't say anything, it was dark in the room, and Joe wasn't even looking my way, when he suddenly said, "I feel dizzy right here." I said I was feeling the same way, but as soon as we left that area of the room the feeling passed.

We taped a few white spots moving around directly over the bed. One of their cats, who previously had acted very nervous and kept running from room to room, jumped onto the bed and proceeded to lay down right where the spots had appeared. The cat now seemed quite calm and relaxed, and more than content to remain there.

As the four of us then moved down the hallway toward Joe's old bedroom (the site of the glowing man and hand under the bed), we all heard a scratching sound coming from the room. It was too heavy and loud to be produced by a cat (and the only cat in the house was still on the bed in the other room). It sounded like a dog's claws scratching on a door. When we entered the room the sound stopped, and we opened the closet doors but found nothing. This was particularly unusual for two reasons—they don't own a dog, and the sound was not recorded by the camcorder! I had been holding the camcorder and was the first to enter the room, so the sensitive microphone should have picked up the sounds that everyone else behind me in the hallway all heard clearly. What is usually the case is that the camcorder picks up sounds we didn't hear at the time, and I just can't understand how it didn't get this distinct scratching noise.

Nothing else unusual happened in that room, and we even checked under the beds just to be sure! We moved on to the oldest bedroom in Goshen—the room that was constructed as part of the 1740 house. Kathy was last in line into the room, and just before entering she heard a whispered voice behind her. She turned, thinking it was one of her daughters, but no one was there.

Once inside, we taped a long, thin wispy shape that appeared to move from near the bed in front of us, up and to our right. A few moments later an icy cold breeze whipped around us. No windows were open, and that was no draft. It went by with force and was so cold it gave me goosebumps and sent a shiver up my spine. This is the room where Kathy's father felt as if he was being pushed down into the bed, and it was no wonder why he wouldn't sleep in there again.

Our final stop was the basement. I had forgotten to switch off the record button on the camcorder, so I ended up taping my feet as we made our way down the stairs. Normally, I would be annoyed by such extraneous "footage," but this time I was glad the camera was running. As Joe, Kathy and Bob examined the section of the basement to the right of the stairs, I went by myself to the left. It was an open area, and even in the darkness I could see the old stone foundation. As I walked slowly forward the camera captured my feet hesitating for just a second, because at that moment I saw something that made my heart skip a beat. Okay, several beats.

Peering through the darkness, I thought I saw the outline of a human figure. It was black and over five feet tall, and right in front of me up against the stone wall. Could this be the Dark Man? In the span of less than a second, I realized the figure had a grotesque head and large, disfigured hands. I couldn't believe my eyes! It was so solid, so real, so horrifying, and so very close. My thoughts raced—it has to be real—but how could it be real—but if it is real, I'm in serious trouble…

In a few hundredths of a second, my mind had to decide whether my body would scream and run, or stand its ground and face this hideous apparition. Then my eye caught the noose around its neck, and I saw that the horrible face and hands looked a lot like rubber, and I finally realized this was some kind of Halloween decoration! All of these thoughts sped through my mind as the camcorder taped the moment's hesitation of my feet, then a sharp sigh of relief as I announced I had discovered their little friend.

It was then Joe and Kathy's turn to be horrified, because they had meant to take their Halloween witch down and put it away before we arrived. They began to apologize profusely for unintentionally scaring the life out of me, but we all started laughing so hard it was difficult to speak. Within a single footstep, it became both the scariest and funniest moment in my ghost investigating career.

However, the laughter ended as abruptly as it began, when Bob said, "Take a look at your Halloween witch, now!"

He had decided to take some digital images of the witch as soon as he saw it. Nothing unusual appeared. However, he took another after we started laughing and suddenly the entire area around the witch was covered in those strange white orbs. I put the camcorder on the tripod and we taped in infrared for a while, and captured many small white lights. Had we attracted something by the change in our energy level when we started laughing?

Whatever is happening in that basement, I now have a new request to the owners of a haunted residence: Would you please remove all Halloween decorations before I get there! My heart can't stand many more episodes like that.

The next day I made a copy of our camcorder footage

The Halloween witch surrounded by orbs.

and mailed it to Joe and Kathy. Many of their friends and family were understandably anxious to view it. A few days later I received an e-mail saying the tape hadn't arrived yet, which was ridiculous because we only lived a few miles apart. Another week passed, and still no tape. Finally, I made another tape and personally drove over to the house and handed it to Kathy. The next day the tape showed up in the mail—18 days after it was sent. It seemed very strange, but I guess we all knew that nothing is normal where the post office is concerned. Whether or not it's paranormal is for you to decide.

It is also strange to note that Joe decided to get his own camcorder to try to capture on tape the many little white spots we recorded that night. After a couple of months of trying, he has yet to tape a single orb, streak or spot! If these objects had simply been dust or airborne particles, why were they only in the air when we were there? Perhaps whatever it really was had obliged Joe's request to put on a good show for us.

Or, perhaps, much of the paranormal energy that was there has gone. Soon after our visit, they contacted psychic Thomas Ellis and requested a spiritual clearing, which he performed from his home in Ohio. Thomas did find quite a list of entities and unusual energies in the house—including those of both men and women, as well as an energy portal between worlds—and believed he was successful in "returning it all to the light." While some strange things still occur in the house, it has been relatively quiet since the clearing.

(It is also interesting to note that Kathy was not aware of when Thomas had planned to perform his clearing, but as she sat at the computer one afternoon a sudden wave of sadness swept over her and she began to cry. She felt a sense of desolation, like being completely alone, or leaving a place to which you were attached. Later that day, she found out in Thomas' e-mail that these feelings coincided exactly with the time the clearing had begun.)

Bob and I returned on July 31, 2002 to see just how things had changed in the house. On our first visit, there was a tangible energy that put everyone on edge. This time, however, it felt like a "normal" house—calm, with nothing seemingly out of the ordinary.

When we started up the cameras, Joe's freshly-recharged battery in his camcorder was inexplicably dead, but once we got started everything worked fine. Although, unlike our first visit, we didn't see or hear anything out of the ordinary. Neither the digital camera, nor the camcorders taping in infrared, captured any streaks, orbs, darting lights or sounds.

However, far from being disappointed, I was actually quite pleased. Had the white spots and orbs we captured on our first visit been caused by dust or insects, or some other natural objects, at least some should have appeared during our second visit. I feel their complete absence the second time adds considerable credibility to the original evidence.

The next day as Joe and I were discussing our findings (or lack thereof) his phone started hissing and clicking. The cordless phone had never given him any problems, but now its battery acted is if it, too, was dying. While all phone batteries eventually need to be replaced, it was odd that it chose our conversation about ghosts in the house as the time to die.

Several days before our second visit, Kathy had thrown a surprise 40th birthday party for Joe. One man who attended said to them, "You know they aren't gone." When they asked him to explain what he meant, he described several entities he "saw" in the house. He said they were all still there, but they were no longer making their presence known because they didn't want to be driven from the house. This man was previously aware of the ghost stories about the house, and some of the things he described could be the result of this prior knowledge and a good imagination, or he may truly be sensitive. In any case, regardless of whether the spirits of the old farmhouse are gone or simply dormant, things are not what they used to be there.

While Kathy and Joe say they kind of miss the spirits, I adamantly maintain that this is a very good thing for all involved. For Joe and Kathy, there is more than enough to occupy them in life, without having to deal with the troubles of the dead. For their three young daughters, hopefully they will all be spared the terror that Joe experienced as a child. And last, but certainly not least, the spirits themselves may have finally found some degree of peace.

The Trolley View Farm is a nice place to spend your life, but I wouldn't want to spend eternity there…

Home for Aged Women

Mike Worden's sister-in-law, Marie, was walking one afternoon with her 2-year-old daughter down a street in Port Jervis, New York, when they passed a large old house that had been vacant for eight years. The house had a central portion, with a long two-story wing stretching off to one side, which had been used as a "Home for Aged Women." Marie thought that with some creativity and effort it would make a beautiful home for her family. *If only it was for sale*, she thought.

The next day, Marie was reading the local newspaper, when her eye caught an announcement about the sale of some city property. There, in the list of properties, was the vacant home for aged women! Less than twenty-four hours after she had wished for the house to come up for sale, it was on the market. Marie and her husband, Tony, made their offer, it was accepted, and the closing took place on her birthday.

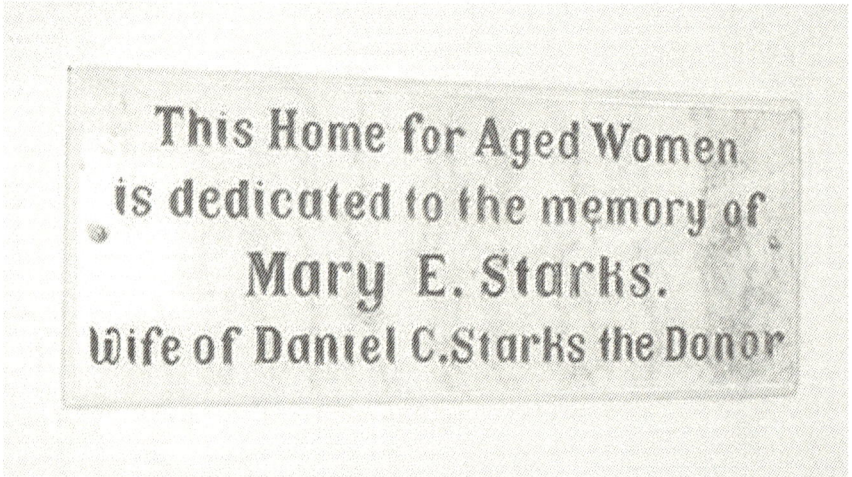

This Home for Aged Women is dedicated to the memory of Mary E. Starks. Wife of Daniel C. Starks the Donor

This marble plaque still hangs on the wall of the first floor hallway.

With more than two dozen rooms on two floors, a basement, and attic, bringing the house back to its former glory was going to take a lot of time and money. Fortunately, Marie and Tony had renovated other houses, and could do much of the work themselves. One job they left to the professionals, however, was the plumbing.

Marie could not be there when the work was being done, so when the plumber and his assistant arrived, they were the only two people in the sprawling house. Or so they thought. While they were working in the basement, the assistant commented that the owners had just arrived. The plumber told him that couldn't be true, because he knew that Marie and Tony had other commitments that day. The other man insisted that he

56

clearly heard not one, but several people walking around on the first floor above them. If it wasn't the owners, then someone else was definitely in the house.

When the man persisted in his claims that they were not alone, the plumber finally decided they had better take a look. Perhaps someone had broken into the house? The two men searched every room, from top to bottom, but found no one. However, even though it became evident that they were the only two living people in the house, the assistant remained certain about what he had heard.

Marie was not happy about the report of the phantom occupants, because she, too, had heard strange things. Many times when she was working alone in the house, it sounded as if other people were there. She tried to convince herself it was just normal "old house sounds," but they became harder and harder to explain away, and she admits she "got the spooks" quite often. As the inexplicable occurrences continued, Marie finally had to accept the possibility that the sounds may be the result of "other reasons." Perhaps the old ladies hadn't yet left the building?

One of the long hallways, containing small bedrooms on both sides.

Bob and I arranged to meet Mike, Autumn and Marie at the house in March of 2002. At the time, Bob and I were doing some work on a few rooms in our own house, and were moderately overwhelmed by the task. When we entered Marie's house with its dozens of rooms, it made our heads spin to think of what was involved renovating a structure of that size.

Since the place has so many rooms, before setting up any equipment we decided we needed to get our bearings. Marie showed us the large living room and family room which were almost complete, the large bedrooms on the second floor, and then the two floors of small bedrooms that lined the hallways running the length of that wing of the house. The garage still contained a pair of classic Cadillacs left (for what reason?) by the previous owners. The basement had a maze of rooms, with the furnace room being one place that always gave Marie a severe case of "the creeps."

It was in the basement where I first mentioned that I smelled the scent of a floral perfume. Everyone else said that they had also smelled it in different parts of the house. After a quick sniff check of each other, we agreed it wasn't any perfume, cologne, or anything we had on. It was also obvious that the musty basement of a house that was vacant for almost a decade should not be the source of any heavy floral scent. Mike put it best by describing it as "an old lady perfume" smell. Perhaps it was.

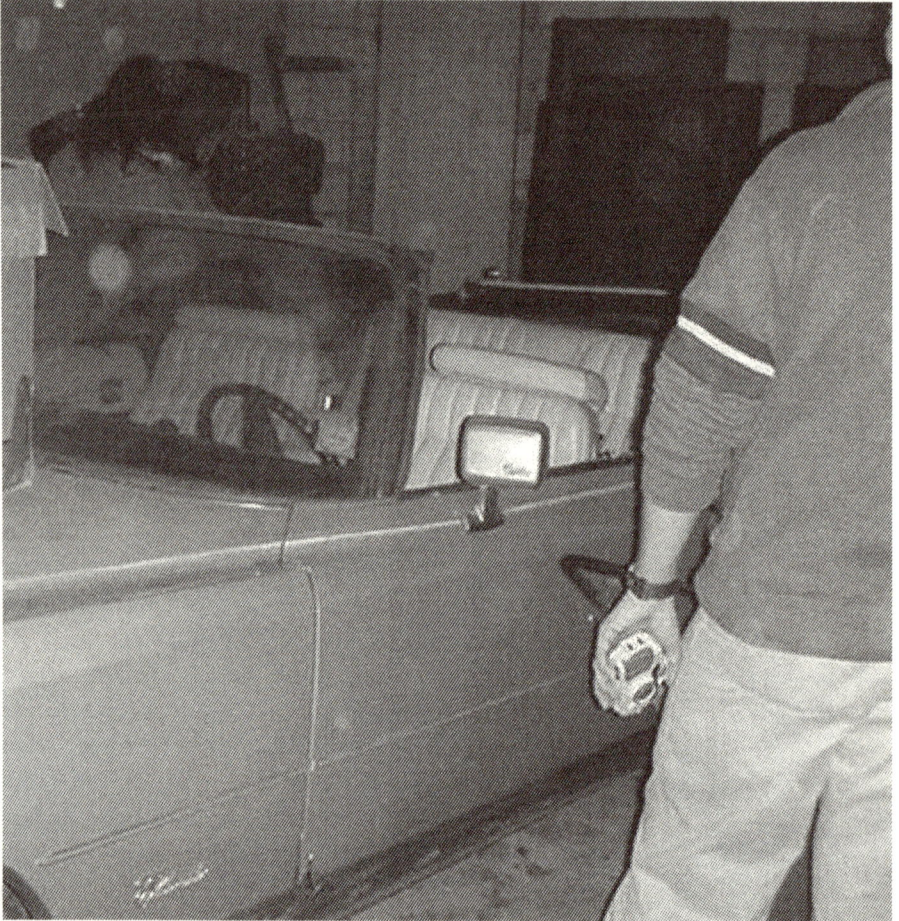

It was actually in the garage where I felt the strongest presence. That presence seemed to be near a dresser at the far end of the garage. I asked Bob to take a picture in that direction. Many of those mysterious orbs showed up. While the argument could be made that the orbs appearing on the Cadillac are the result of reflections, I doubt that the back of Mike's shirt and pants were also reflecting. A few orbs appear in the air at the back of the garage as well. There wasn't any dust on the lens, and this profusion of orbs did not appear on any of the other dozens of photos. I don't know what causes this effect, but they certainly liked Mike!

We decided that we would place our camcorder facing down the hall of bedrooms on the first floor and let the tape run for a while. Mike's camcorder would be set up in the basement, with cables running upstairs to a monitor in the living room. This way we could observe the area without disturbing it by kicking up dust, making noises, etc.

Marie and Autumn stayed on the first floor, as Mike, Bob and I went down to the basement to find the best location to set up the camcorder. As we stood in the central room, we all heard footsteps directly over our heads in the hallway, moving away from the staircase. The person was wearing hard-soled shoes, and the distinctive footsteps were so clear and so close, we didn't suspect anything unusual. We naturally assumed it was Marie or Autumn walking around. No big deal.

However, when we came upstairs, we found the two women near the kitchen in the back of the house, and I noticed both were wearing soft-soled shoes. Before I could say anything, Marie asked if one of us had come up the stairs a few minutes earlier. We explained that it wasn't any of us, and then asked if either of them had been walking across the floor near the staircase. They said that they had been standing on the same spot the entire time we were in the basement.

Once we sorted everything out, it seemed that as Marie and Autumn stood near the kitchen, they heard someone, with hard-soled shoes, coming up the basement stairs to the first floor, but didn't see anyone step into the hallway and didn't hear anymore footsteps. Just as they ceased to hear the footsteps, Mike, Bob and I heard someone step from the top of the staircase and walk down the hall.

We didn't hear anyone on the stairs, and they didn't hear anyone in the hall, but putting both experiences together, it appears as if someone came up out of the basement and went down the hall of the first floor, making certain to not give away their presence to anyone close. I suddenly had great sympathy for the poor plumber's assistant, and knew exactly how he felt as several phantom residents walked the floors above him.

Had we left at that point, I would have considered the investigation a success, but the fun in the basement was just beginning. Mike placed his camcorder at the bottom of the basement stairs, facing into the central room. As we watched from the living room, we saw a few little white spots darting by, but nothing too dramatic. Then he and Bob went back downstairs to move the camcorder into the furnace room. Everything looked good on the monitor, until they came upstairs, when the picture went dark.

They went back downstairs again, and before they even reached the camcorder, the picture returned to the monitor in the living room. On the camcorder's tape, the picture was never interrupted, and you can hear Bob and Mike checking the infrared light, cables and connections. Everything seemed fine—until they came back upstairs.

As soon as they returned to the living room, the monitor once again went blank. This time Mike and I headed down the stairs, and as soon as we reached the basement, Bob yelled that the picture had returned. We yelled back that we hadn't done anything, yet. We were still fifteen or twenty feet away from the camcorder, which was in the furnace room off to our right. When we reached the camcorder, everything was running and recording just fine. As we were trying to solve what we thought was a technical problem, there was a sound behind us that made us freeze in our tracks.

Back by the staircase we had just come down, there was a loud scraping or dragging sound. Mike said it made his hair stand on end, and I could feel the goose bumps springing up across both of my arms. There we were in the darkness of the basement of a house where many elderly ladies had probably passed away, and something unseen was dragging a heavy object across the floor just a few yards away from us.

We didn't move, or breathe, for a few moments, but there were no more sounds. We decided to move the camera back into that center room, this time facing the staircase, which was definitely a hot spot of activity. Once again, the picture on the monitor was fine, until we went upstairs. As soon as we went in the living room, the picture disappeared. Apparently, someone was playing tricks, and wanted us in that basement. However, we had enough of those games, and it was three strikes and we were out of there. Mike moved his camcorder to the second floor, where everything worked perfectly, and there were no further interruptions.

Marie had told us an interesting story about one of the large bedrooms on the second floor in the main section of the house. For some reason, every time she brought her little daughter to the house, the girl would run up to this bedroom and close herself in the closet. She wasn't interested in any other closet in the house, just this one. She would spend long

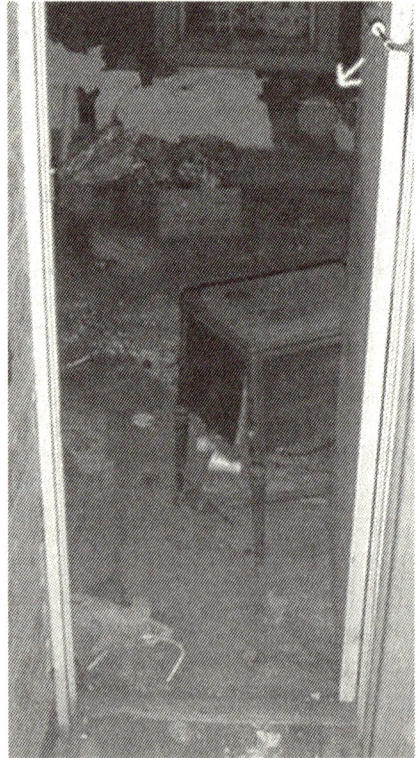

The view of the central room of the basement at the bottom of the stairs. A lot of footsteps and strange sounds are heard here. One large orb is in the background.

periods of time inside laughing and playing by herself. When a friend brought a small boy to visit, he also ran upstairs and closed himself in this same closet. What is the attraction here? When the children are laughing and talking inside, are they truly alone?

We photographed the closet in infrared and in regular light, and we took EMF readings and the temperature. Nothing seemed out of the ordinary. But we did not have the eyes of children, who are often sensitive to things adults can't see. Of course, they also have vivid imaginations, and often invent playmates. Did this closet hold something paranormal, or was it simply an empty closet in which children imagined their own world?

With a complete lack of any physical evidence, I came to the conclusion that sometimes a closet is just a closet. Then in August, as I prepared to write this story, I played back the audio tape from the tape recorder I had carried around the house. I hadn't listened to it sooner because I usually rely on video for both images and sound, and just use the tape recorder as a hands-free way to keep notes during an investigation.

On the tape, Bob, Mike, Marie, her mother (who had arrived shortly before), and I were speaking about the closet in that room. As Bob took some digital photos, Mike left to get his camcorder. We are all speaking in normal voices—if anything, a little louder than normal as we were not standing close together. Marie was about fifteen feet from me (and the tape recorder), and just as she is commenting, "If there is someone in the closet, it must be someone friendly," there is a whispered voice very close to the tape recorder. It sounds like a female voice whispering, "There she is."

I was startled when I first heard it. I played it back over and over again, and tried to reconstruct the scene of who was where at the time. Bob, Marie and her mother were near the closet. I was at the other end of the room, and Mike was in a different part of the house. No one was whispering, and no one that I could see was near me.

A popular trend in ghost hunting in recent years is EVP, or Electronic Voice Phenomena. I think of it more as Erroneous Voice Phenomena, as computer-enhanced hisses and scratches on audio tapes are interpreted as coherent sentences. There are many web sites on the Internet that contain examples to which you can listen, and they not only give the sound, they provide their "translation." Feel free to knock yourself out and listen to a few hundred examples, but I have yet to hear a single one that sounds like legitimate spoken words. In fact, try not to read the interpretation before listening, as the suggestion of words could influence you. Just click on something and see if you come up with anything resembling what they contend it is.

Like computer-enhanced images, my feeling about EVP is that if you don't get a clear voice on tape that doesn't require any manipulation, you don't have valid evidence. I would love to be proven wrong in this case, and I am always hopeful when I listen to new examples, but I have always been disappointed.

That being said, could the whispered voice that I think is saying, "There she is," be the result of brushing the microphone of the tape recorder against something, or just some static or inconsistency in the tape itself? Absolutely. In fact, Bob has listened to the sound and doesn't think it is a voice or words. However, in all my years of ghost investigating, I've never recorded anything like this. Without any enhancing or manipulating, and doing nothing more than hitting the Play button, it sure sounds to me like a woman's voice whispering.

If, then, we go on the premise that this *was* a voice, and it did say, "There she is," it begs the questions *who* is she, and *where* is she? Not to mention who was it that spoke the words. The fact that Marie was talking about the possibility of someone friendly being in the closet, tends to make me think that the voice and the closet are connected. Was a helpful spirit pointing out a woman or female child in the closet, one that we were unable to see? Or was the voice pointing out one of the living women in the room, which at that point was either Marie, her mother, or me.

Lots of questions. Lots of speculation. Not many answers. Such is often the nature of a ghost investigation. Until the spirits start providing names, dates and places, in clear, unmistakable voices, we will have to keep trying to put together the few pieces of puzzle as best we can.

What I can say from our experience is that it is likely that the elderly ladies who ended their days in this house have not yet ended their occupancy. The sound of footsteps and the smell of perfume may be signs that these women don't quite know they are dead, or simply refuse to leave. The mischievous activity and unusual attraction to the closet (as well as the possible whispered voice) may indicate that the spirits of children are also present. Over 100 years of history can provide quite a few ghosts.

Marie and Tony continue to work on the house, and they are now at the stage where they are preparing to knock down some walls in the wing of small bedrooms. As renovations of this nature can stir up paranormal activity, Marie did comment that she wonders if this will "bring people out of the woodwork"—literally. Hopefully, the old ladies, and whoever else may still walk the halls (and closets) will appreciate the efforts to restore their former home. And, hopefully, once Marie and her family move in, the wandering spirits will understand that it's time for them to move on.

Gettysburg

England is often referred to as the most haunted country in the world. However, even that ghost-filled island nation would be hard pressed to find a single town that is more haunted than the small Pennsylvania community that was the site of one of the greatest human dramas in history. To fully appreciate what happened at Gettysburg, and what remains there today, you must walk its fields, spend the night in one of its old homes and sit atop a hill and silently watch the sun set. Gettysburg is a place that must be experienced—as no words or pictures can ever accurately describe the feelings that sweep over you there.

Years before I became the Ghost Investigator, I wrote and lectured about the Civil War (and I still do). I have always been fascinated by military history, in part because my father was a Marine in World War II and the Korean War, and I wanted to understand as best as I could what he experienced. The other reason has to do with why Chaucer, Shakespeare and Jane Austin are my favorite authors—they were masters of portrayals of the full spectrum of human nature, and as a skilled author does for his characters, so too, does war expose the best and worst of mankind.

If you had to choose only one war in which to study extraordinary courage, devotion and self-sacrifice, as well as the depths of suffering and anguish, the Civil War would be an excellent choice. And if you could only choose one battle of the Civil War to study, Gettysburg would be the obvious choice. Due to its massive scale, the pivotal importance of the outcome, the staggering number of casualties and the relationships and interactions of the combatants, this battle contained an intense concentration of human emotions that can still be sensed to this day.

On my first visit to Gettysburg, I was prepared for an historical overload, knowing there would be so much more than I could absorb and appreciate in a single visit. What I had not been prepared for, was the solemn and almost reverent atmosphere that I had previously only experienced in European cathedrals which were the sites of hundreds of years of worship. At first this was startling, but the more I reflected upon it, the more it made sense. In addition to all that had occurred during the actual battle, veterans and visitors have flocked to Gettysburg ever since in what really amounts to a kind of pilgrimage.

After returning from my trip, I described my battlefield-cathedral analogy to a friend, and admittedly she thought I was way off base. But she has never been there, and for those of you who have visited and gotten away from the fast food restaurants, souvenir shops and crowds to some quiet spot on the battlefield, you know what I mean. You cannot stand on Little Round Top, or walk across the field of Pickett's Charge, or look down the long rows of unknown soldiers in the National Cemetery without feeling that *something* else is there.

Unfortunately, however, much of what is there should have moved on in 1863. There are countless reports of ghostly soldiers across the battlefield, in the streets of town, and in the old farmhouses that served as field hospitals. In addition to spirits directly linked to the battle, there are other stories involving townspeople—predominantly women and children—who for a variety of reasons are still seen at the sites of their deaths or some other tragic event. It is actually difficult to find a 19th century building or section of the battlefield that is *not* reputed to be haunted.

While I could relate dozens of popular stories I have heard or read about, I would prefer to describe unusual events with which I have had personal experience. I have been going to Gettysburg regularly over the past ten years—initially as a tourist, then to do book signings at the battlefield preservation book shows, and to lecture on two occasions during the Gettysburg Heritage Days (which are at the end of June and beginning of July, so they include the anniversary dates of the battle). Over the past decade I have covered a lot of square feet of battlefield and have encountered several odd things.

The first occurred in the mid-1990s when Bob Strong and I took a tour of the Farnsworth House in town. The Farnsworth still has several bullet holes from the battle in its brick walls, and Confederate sharpshooters used the top floor of the home to fire upon Union troops. It is believed that the stray shot that killed Jenny Wade—the only Gettysburg resident to be killed in the battle—was fired from the Farnsworth. (Yes, Jenny Wade's ghost has been seen at her home.)

Now a bed and breakfast, restaurant and bookshop, the Farnsworth nonetheless still looks much as it did during the battle on July 1, 2 and 3 in 1863. There is also a famous photograph taken in November of that year in which the Farnsworth can be seen in the background. The photo captured the official procession making its way to the dedication of the new National Cemetery, where Lincoln was to deliver his famous Gettysburg Address.

In addition to all of the wonderful history connected with this house, there appears to be other connections—those to the other world. As many as fourteen different ghosts have been seen and felt there, and if you want to hear about them, you can attend one of the evening ghost story presentations, which are held in the Farnsworth's spooky basement. If you want to have the chance to possibly experience their ghosts firsthand, stay in one of their guest rooms in the main part of the house.

The Farnsworth House as it looks today.

In all fairness, I have to say that I had heard that the Farnsworth was supposed to be haunted, but as I had no idea at that point that I would someday be writing ghost books and conducting investigations, my focus of the tour was purely for the history. And there was certainly nothing spooky about the circumstances of the tour—a lot of people packed together moving slowly through the narrow hallways and staircases. In the crowd, Bob and I had become separated, and he was about fifteen people ahead of me as we inched step by step up the main staircase. The tour guide, who was at the front of the line on the second floor, then asked everyone to stop where they were, so she could relay some more information. I was beginning to think the tour was not such a great idea, until I stepped onto the landing in the middle of the staircase, next to where an old grandfather clock stands.

Suddenly I felt as if the floor under my feet was shifting, and I moved back and forth to try to regain my balance. I also felt very disoriented—as if I had actually walked into another place or time. This was unlike anything I had ever experienced, and I was beginning to think something must be wrong with my inner ear or nervous system. Then our tour guide pointed directly toward me and said, "On that landing many people have seen the ghost of a Confederate soldier standing by the clock."

That snapped me out of it a bit, and then the line lurched forward. At the instant my feet were on the next step, the feeling was gone completely.

65

However, I didn't have long to question my sanity, for as I reached the second floor, I felt compelled to quickly turn around and look behind me, because I had the strong feeling that a woman in the hallway was trying to get my attention. There was no one there, but as everyone else on line faced the guide, and I was looking in the opposite direction down the small hallway, I heard her say, "And down that hallway has appeared the spirit of a woman."

By this point I was fairly staggering. When we finally made it up to the attic I caught up with Bob, grabbed his arm and told him what had just happened. Rather than question my sanity, he commented on how neat he thought it was. That convinced him then and there that someday we would have to spend the night at the Farnsworth.

We had that opportunity a year or two later. However, absolutely nothing happened during our stay. We both slept soundly and didn't feel anything unusual, but that would not be the case the next time we went to the Farnsworth. I was giving a lecture that year on Civil War humor, and my mind was on my notes, not ghosts. Civil War historians and enthusiasts really know their stuff, and you can't stand up in front of an auditorium full of them and not have all of your facts pinned down.

We were staying in a room around the corner from the small hallway where I had sensed the woman. Thankfully, I slept undisturbed all night. However, just about dawn I suddenly awoke and sat up in bed. The room was very faintly lit and there were no sounds. Although I couldn't physically see or hear anything, I had the distinct impression that a woman in a 19th century dress was standing next to the bed. She was very upset and the feeling of grief was intense. It's hard to say how long this persisted—30 seconds, perhaps a minute or two—and then the feeling and the image faded and seemed to recede toward the door until it was completely gone.

While I try to deal in scientific evidence, or phenomena that are more concrete in order to avoid possible interference by my imagination, these episodes were so clear and distinct that they were impossible to ignore. Even though I have no photos, EMF readings or any tangible proof that the Farnsworth House is haunted by at least two ghosts, I have been more than convinced. But by all means, don't take my word for it. Make some reservations and be sure to ask for one of the haunted rooms. Go with an open mind and no expectations, and try to keep your imagination in check. If you are sensitive to such things, you might just have an experience that will convince you, too.

Fortunately, not all of the things we have encountered in Gettysburg have been so invisible. On one July 2 afternoon (the anniversary of the second day of the battle), Bob and I were exploring the areas where the battles had raged on that day, and we tried to be at the sites during the actual times they had taken place. As we were approaching the Wheatfield (a place where the fighting was so deadly a soldier commented that you could walk its entire length on bodies and never touch the ground), we both saw a man dressed in a Confederate uniform in the middle of the large open field, perhaps about 200 feet away. His musket was on his right shoulder and he was slowly walking west, right toward us.

This appeared to be nothing out of the ordinary. In Gettysburg there are often more men dressed in Civil War uniforms (and women in hoop skirts) than there are in jeans and T-shirts, especially when reenactments are taking place during the Heritage Days. What was a little unusual was how this soldier appeared. Everything about him seemed to be too bright and shiny in the late afternoon sun—as if everything he was wearing was reflecting light. I joked to Bob that a good Confederate reenactor shouldn't have such a highly polished weapon or accoutrements. He should be somewhat ragged and dirty to be accurate.

At that time I was working on an article about reenactors, so Bob suggested that we stop and talk to this man, despite how clean and bright he looked. I thought it was a good idea, so I reached down to the floor of the van for the bag that held my camera and note pad, while Bob pulled over into the parking area. When I sat back up after no more than five seconds, the soldier was gone.

"Where did he go?" I asked Bob, puzzled but not yet suspicious.

"I don't know!" he replied. "Where could he have gone?"

I suggested that perhaps he had tripped and fallen down, or had just decided to sit down and rest. We thought that those were the only two possibilities as he was in the middle of an open field at one instant, and was nowhere to be seen in the next. We got out of the van and started walking toward the spot where we had last seen him. We found nothing.

"This is ridiculous! This doesn't make any sense! Where did he go?" we both asked as we zigzagged across the field looking for that Confederate soldier.

After a few minutes we hurried back to the van and followed the road around the Wheatfield a couple of times. There was absolutely no one. Bob and I each described what we had seen, and we both did see the same exact thing—a man in a Confederate uniform carrying a gun on his shoulder and appearing to be very bright, who somehow managed to vanish from an open field in a matter of seconds. It was a hard thing to fathom, and to this day whenever anyone asks me if I have ever seen an actual apparition in human form, I always reply that I *think* I *might* have glimpsed one that day in Gettysburg.

Of course, we were at the Wheatfield on the anniversary day of the battle, at the exact time the battle was taking place, and both sides did suffer terrible casualties, so if the ghost of a Confederate soldier was going to make an appearance, this would have been as good a time as any! If only I had some idea that we were witnessing something unusual, I would not have taken my eyes off of him for a second, but that is the nature of things. You can sit all night at a haunted site with cameras rolling and get squat, or you can be driving through a battlefield on a sunny day not expecting anything, and have an apparition walk straight towards you!

The sign describing the battle at the Wheatfield stands close to where we were when we witnessed the Confederate soldier in the middle of this field. As you can see, there is nowhere a person could hide.

Just a few years ago, we were driving along the Emmitsburg Road, which cuts between the fields over which thousands of Confederate soldiers marched and died during Pickett's Charge. (Yes, I know that technically this battle should be referred to as Longstreet's Assault, but most people are familiar with the popular name.) It was July 3, the anniversary of the tragic, failed attack, and it was once again during the afternoon hours when the battle had taken place.

For no apparent reason one of the cars ahead of us suddenly stopped in the middle of the road, as did the car heading the opposite direction. Bob and I had our fill of Gettysburg traffic that day and we both said, "Great, now what's the problem?" Then we noticed three men (who were definitely alive!) dressed in Confederate uniforms, marching deliberately and with great determination across the field to our left, from the direction where Pickett's Charge began. The man in the center was carrying a large Confederate flag and it was clear they intended to cross the road and continue on to the stone wall, as the actual soldiers had tried to do during the battle.

I admit, we were both annoyed that traffic had stopped so they could march uninterrupted across the road and onto the other section of the field. Being northerners who are somewhat less than sympathetic to the southern cause, we probably even let a disparaging remark or two slip out. However, as we watched these men approach the road, we both fell silent.

I could sense the pride with which these men marched forward, and recalled what had been taking place at that very moment on that exact spot over 130 years ago. Something hit me—hard. As they crossed the road onto the next field, it felt as if thousands of souls marched with them, and the feeling swept over me and made a chill run up my spine.

When the line of cars began to move again, the spell was broken, but I realized my eyes were full of tears. I was afraid to turn back and face Bob because I didn't want him to see me crying over what I was sure to him was just a few rebel reenactors tying up traffic. Finally, I tried to discreetly wipe away the tears and then looked over at him, and saw that he was misty eyed, too! He was just as choked up as I was, and it took us a minute to finally describe what we had both felt. Even as I write about this years later, my eyes get moist and I can clearly recall that overpowering feeling sweeping over us. Devotion and sacrifice do indeed leave deep and lasting impressions.

After regaining my composure, I snapped this picture of the three men (slightly right of center, carrying the flag) marching across the field toward the wall where Union defenders repulsed Confederate soldiers during Pickett's Charge. One can only imagine what it was like walking across an open field into the face of musket and cannon fire. Remarkably, it took years for generals to realize that the technology of the weaponry made this attack strategy obsolete and suicidal. Even in WWI, men went "over the top" into machine gun fire.

69

I experienced a similar feeling on another occasion, but not nearly as intense. I was in Gettysburg to give a lecture on the soldiers and chaplain of the 17th Connecticut Regiment of Volunteer Infantry. The lecture took place in the auditorium of the middle school, which is right next to the area where one of the two monuments dedicated to the 17th CT stands. During the lecture, I was cognizant of the fact that I was talking about men who fought and died on that very spot, yet it was basically an intellectual understanding. It didn't hit me in the gut until the next day when we went to photograph the monument.

As we stood next to the slender obelisk, I recited from memory part of the oration delivered by Reverend Alexander Ramsay Thompson when the monument was dedicated in October of 1889.

Your valor, your purpose, your endurance, your privations in camp and march and field, your honorable wounds, the life devoted of your comrades were not in vain. The nation is one. Long after this memorial stone shall have crumbled, the generations to come will apprehend results that came of this mighty struggle in a united country, and a beneficent government and a prosperous people...

The monument dedicated to the 17th CT at the base of Cemetery Hill. There is another 17th CT monument on Barlow's Knoll.

As I spoke his words aloud, there was that telltale tingling sensation you get when you know you are not alone. While I don't believe the entire regiment was there, I do feel there was someone who appreciated my acknowledging what these men had done.

One of the few times we were actually looking for paranormal activity in Gettysburg was when we went to the Triangular Field, which is behind Devil's Den to the west. I had read that cameras and electrical equipment regularly malfunction there, and that many strange things are seen and heard. On one of our trips we decided to see if there was any truth to these stories.

If you have ever been to Gettysburg in July, you know how brutally hot it is, and the day we went to the Triangular Field was no exception. The sun was unrelenting and we had done most of our touring that day in the comfort of the air conditioned car. So we had the irrational hope that if any of our cameras were going to refuse to work, they would do so without us having to walk too far in the field in that heat.

In reality, we walked back and forth across the field taking pictures with no problems. Still, I couldn't be disappointed because the history of the place was so fascinating. When the heat finally overcame the fascination, we headed back toward the car. We were walking along a path when my left hand passed through a patch of cold air. I walked a few more feet and thought, "Wait just one minute! How can anything out here be cold in this hellish heat?"

The gate that opens into the Triangular Field.
The cold spot was down the path near the tree line.

I told Bob to stop and went back to the spot. Holding my hand out over the area, it felt like I had just stuck my hand into a refrigerator. Bob held his hand out, too, and also said that the air felt very cold, at least forty degrees colder than the upper ninety-degree temperature on the rest of the field. I examined the ground and kicked the dirt a bit to see if there was some kind of cover or grating over an underground water source or tunnel, but there was nothing but solid ground that appeared to be no different than any other part of the field.

We remained there for several minutes and determined the cold spot was roughly four or five feet in diameter and at least as tall as we could reach. Nothing appeared in our photographs, and I did not have any of my instruments with me, but the fact that a patch of the Triangular Field was cold on a hot summer's day was undeniable. It is one of those spots I would recommend you visit, preferably when it is warm. See for yourself if your camera works, or if your hand passes through something cold and inexplicable.

The cold spot (indicated by the arrow), is located where two paths meet. The gate is at the crest of the hill. Devil's Den is on the hill to the right.

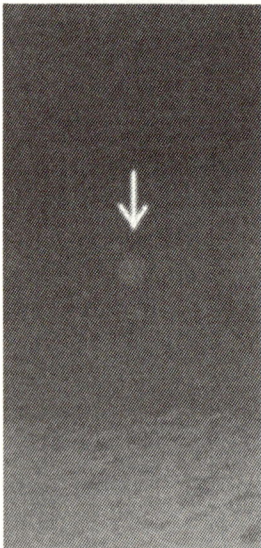

On our visit to Gettysburg in 2002, we took photographs (left) of the Triangular Field at night. These orbs appeared in only one photo—taken at the cold spot.

The last episode I want to describe, I do so with hesitation as it is so bizarre as to sound like a work of fiction. I'm still not sure exactly what happened, or why, but I will present the details and let you make your own judgment.

It was the day before I was to be doing a book signing at one of the shows, and Bob and I were just being tourists for the day. We were on Cemetery Hill reading the plaques and taking some photographs. For some stupid reason, I got it in my head to silently ask if there was any way I could help any spirits who might be there. If anyone wanted to make his plight known to me, I would be happy to be a conduit.

Bad idea. Very bad. A perfect example of being careful what you ask for because you might get it.

A few moments later I had my camera up to my eye and was about to take a photograph. The next thing I knew my body was slamming onto the ground with a painful jolt. Hearing the thud, Bob turned around, saw me on the ground with my hand on my neck and asked what had happened. The very first thing I said was that it felt like I had been shot in the neck—although, I obviously must have simply slipped on something. He looked at the dry, flat ground and made some joke that it must have taken quite an effort to find a way to slip and fall there.

I would have laughed, but as he helped me up the pain in my neck was intense and there was numbness in my face and down the right side of my body. Due to accidents (such as getting rear-ended by three cars on the Westside Highway in Manhattan) I do have trouble with my neck and back, but I knew this was serious and needed immediate attention. I also knew that if I went to the local hospital they would probably give me a brace and some drugs, and I would be useless for a week.

As luck would have it, even though it was the Saturday of a long Fourth of July weekend, a chiropractor in town had office hours. Long story short, I got in to see him and he was impressed by how much damage I had managed to sustain. However, thanks to his skills, the numbness quickly faded, and the pain became manageable. I was able to do the book signing the next day, and with the help of ice packs and ibuprofen, I was almost fully recovered within a few days.

The question remained, however, as to whether I had simply stumbled (although I can't recall that I was even moving at the time), or had I opened my big psychic mouth and paid the price. What I needed to do was find out if there was any record of anyone getting shot in the neck in that area of Cemetery Hill. I knew it would be like a needle in the haystack, but I was determined to the point of obsession. General descriptions of the battle were useless; what I needed was one of those minute-by-minute, detailed accounts of each day of the battle.

After several weeks of searching, I was sitting on the floor of a bookstore going through everything they had on Gettysburg. Picking up one particularly enormous volume, I scanned the index for Cemetery Hill entries and started going over each one. Scanning one of the pages I saw the usual "fierce fighting on Cemetery Hill, etc., etc., many casualties, etc., etc., Colonel Avery shot in the neck…"

My breath caught in my throat as I stared at those words. I went back to the beginning of the page and absorbed every word. Confederate Colonel Isaac Avery of the 6th North Carolina State Troops was shot in the neck and fell from his horse on Cemetery Hill. His right hand was paralyzed, he couldn't speak and he knew he was dying. With rapidly failing strength, he grabbed a twig in his left hand and used his own blood to write a final message before he died. He managed to scribble the words, "Tell my father I died with my face to the enemy." His body was buried, but later attempts to find it to return his remains to North Carolina failed, and it is not known today where his grave is located.

I read that passage over and over again, still not believing what I seeing. In the following weeks I confirmed through different sources that Avery had indeed received a fatal neck wound somewhere very near to where I had fallen and exclaimed that it felt like I had been shot in the neck.

A cannon and monuments on Cemetery Hill.
The famous gate to the Evergreen Cemetery is in the background.

Do I believe for one minute that the ghost of Colonel Avery possessed me or caused me harm? Absolutely not. But it is just possible that tragic events leave some kind of energetic residue or impressions that can be experienced by others. While this would obviously be a far more dramatic example than a picture you get in your mind or a gut feeling, I am not prepared to state that this was merely a coincidence. On the other hand, I could not in good conscience swear under oath that it was not just a coincidence—a truly remarkable one, but a coincidence nonetheless.

For me, I think the most compelling piece of evidence is that I stood on that hill and asked for it (although I was hoping for something more like a misty shape on a photo, or a whisper in my ear), and moments later I was on the ground and in severe pain. The episode certainly compelled me to search for answers, and I did find a poignant story that deserves to be told again and again. If there is one thing I learned from all of this, it's to be extremely careful what you say and think, especially at a haunted site.

As with any investigation or eyewitness account, I present the facts, I give my personal opinion, and then encourage the reader to make up his or her own mind. In the case of Gettysburg, you have the unique opportunity to explore hundreds of reports of hauntings, and perhaps discover a few new ones, as well.

Ghosts or not, I strongly recommend Gettysburg for its incredible history. Take the time to learn about and appreciate the stories of the soldiers who did indeed give the "last full measure of their devotion" on those fields. Understand what was at stake there, and the tremendous courage and fortitude it took to fight a Civil War battle. Think of the veterans who returned year after year to pay their respects to fallen comrades, until they too, became memories.

Gettysburg may not have the stone walls and spires of a cathedral, but it is just as worthy of your prayers, reflection and admiration.

The Lizzie Borden House

There's just something about an ax murder.

If Andrew and Abby Borden had been shot, strangled or poisoned, it is doubtful that the case would have been the sensation it was at the time of the murders on August 4, 1892, and it is very unlikely that it would still hold our fascination today.

Guns and poison are somewhat impersonal, as the killer can accomplish his goal at a distance from his victim. Strangling, while requiring contact, is usually relatively clean. But an ax murder is something special—it is intimately personal—as the murderer is sprayed with the blood and gore the weapon produces as it hacks into the body.

Imagine then, the absolute horror felt throughout Fall River, Massachusetts that day, when two corpses were discovered that had been struck with an ax in their heads and faces a total of thirty times! And when the prime suspect appeared to be a woman, the male victim's own daughter, Lizzie, it must have shaken the citizens' stodgy Victorian sensibilities to their very cores.

In the one hundred and ten years that have elapsed since these terrible crimes, there have been dozens of books and countless articles written. Most conclude that Lizzie was guilty, but many theories of varying credibility also point the bloody finger at the maid, Lizzie's sister, Lizzie's uncle, the local doctor, and an illegitimate son. So much conflicting and inaccurate evidence abounds, that about the only thing we can state with any degree of certainty is that the deaths were not the result of suicides!

Lizzie has reason to smile in this 1893 photo which hangs in her room at the Borden house—just three days earlier she was acquitted of murder and was about to become a very wealthy woman.

Some of the pertinent facts of the case are as follows:

In 1892, Andrew Borden was a seventy-year-old man with a large fortune and Scrooge-like manners. He lived in a modest house without electricity, no hot running water and no flush toilets. A privy in the basement served as the only facilities for family and guests.

The Borden house today.

Andrew was involved in many businesses, as well as real estate, and if a tenant was so much as a day late in paying the rent, he could expect to find his family and belongings out on the street within twenty-four hours. When Andrew's first wife, Sarah, died, he married a woman named Abby to help care for his daughters, Emma and Lizzie. As Lizzie grew to womanhood, she strongly resembled her late mother, and there is speculation that Mr. Borden may have begun committing incest with her.

Abby Borden was not liked by either of her stepdaughters, and in the case of Lizzie, that dislike would be better characterized as hatred. Although Lizzie adored animals, there is a story that one day Lizzie took Abby's cat into the basement and chopped its head off with an ax. Later, perhaps in retribution, Mr. Borden chopped the heads off of all of Lizzie's pigeons. A pattern seems to have been developing. (An interesting note: the Borden family crest contains a gryphon holding a battle ax!)

Testimony at Lizzie's trial indicated that Abby was more than just an annoyance to the Borden sisters. It seems that Mr. Borden had planned to write a will that would have left just $25,000 to each daughter, while the remainder of his $500,000 fortune and all of his property would go to Abby.

The day before the murders, Abby complained to a doctor across the street that everyone in the house was sick because someone was trying to poison them. Of course, no refrigeration and little sanitation in the sweltering summer heat often produced food poisoning during those times. Yet, one druggist claimed that just several days earlier, Lizzie attempted to buy ten cents worth of deadly Prussic acid. Two cents worth was sufficient to kill several people.

Emma Borden was older than Lizzie by nine years. At the time of the murders, she was visiting relatives fifteen miles away in Fairhaven. She had been gone an unusually long time, and upon her return after the murders she was supportive of her accused sister.

The maid, Bridget Sullivan, did not appear to be prone to rages and had no known prior history of violence. There were no reports that she had any particular problems with any family members.

There was also John Morse, the brother of Lizzie's real mother. He had a very good rapport with his two nieces, and would most likely not be happy that they wouldn't be inheriting Andrew's estate.

And then we come to Lizzie. Although not well educated, she seemed to be intelligent, at least enough to teach local Chinese immigrants' children. She was involved in many church organizations, was generally kind to people, and loved animals.

She was also a kleptomaniac—habitually stealing from many of the finest stores. Her father quietly paid the bills, and her illegal hobby was allowed to continue. Lizzie also received unusual attention from her father, and despite his tight purse strings, he bought her a fur coat and sent her to Europe for several months. Some experts claim that both the kleptomania and favoritism could be signs that Lizzie was being abused, but again, this is purely speculation.

So, on the morning of August 4, 1892, as the thermometer already hit the 90 degree mark, rising tensions in the Borden house were about to come to a head—literally. Bridget prepared breakfast, and then went outside and became violently ill. She washed some windows on the first floor and then went upstairs to rest in her third-floor room.

John Morse, who had uncharacteristically arrived the day before unannounced and without luggage, spent the night in the guest bedroom. He had breakfast with Andrew and Abby and left through the side door about 8:45am. His alibi was also uncharacteristically tight—he even remembered the badge number on the hat of the trolley conductor. Generally, one would not notice such things unless trying to establish and alibi.

Andrew Borden left around 9am, leaving Abby, Lizzie, and Bridget alone in the house. Sometime before 9:30am, Abby was in the guest bedroom, when someone she must have known entered the room. She attempted no defense as this person struck her with an ax. When Abby fell face down on the floor, the murderer straddled her body, and continued striking her head with an additional eighteen vicious blows of the ax. The back of her skull was obliterated. Bridget and Lizzie claimed to hear nothing.

About 10:45am, Andrew returned home unexpectedly, as he was not feeling well, either. Bridget let him in the front door. Lizzie claimed to have helped him remove his coat and shoes, put on a cardigan sweater, and stretch out of the sofa in the sitting room. Andrew's body was discovered with his shoes on, his coat folded under his head, and no sweater. Lizzie also said she told her father that Abby had received a note and was out visiting a sick friend. No note, sick friend or delivery person was ever located. Lizzie then claims she went into the barn to eat pears and look for lead to make fishing sinkers, although her footprints did not appear on the dusty barn floor.

Some time between 11:00-11:15am, the killer, who had apparently remained undetected in the house for over an hour and a half and had no desire to harm Lizzie or Bridget, stepped through the dining room doorway and swung the ax down into the face of Andrew Borden. Blood spattered all over the wall and doorway as the killer continued smashing the ax through his skull a total of eleven times.

These gruesome murders were overkill—this was something personal.

The location of the sofa (not original) where Andrew Borden was murdered. It is believed that the killer stood in the doorway of the dining room (left).

Soon after, Lizzie called up to Bridget announcing that her father had been killed, and to go for help. When Bridget returned, Lizzie told her to look upstairs in the guest bedroom for Abby. (Why hadn't she told her to look first in Abby's room?) The police arrived about half an hour later, and by the end of the day, thousands of people had gathered in the streets as news of the terrible crimes spread like wildfire.

To say the ensuing investigation was bungled is a gross understatement, as dozens of people entered the house and quickly contaminated the crime scene. Even though Bridget was in the house during both murders, she was "just a servant," and the police never considered her to be a suspect. Therefore, just hours after the murders she was allowed to leave the house with a bundle that wasn't even searched. Over the next few days, she came and went several times—again, never being searched. Only some of Lizzie's clothing and personal items were searched, as it was considered inappropriate at the time to be too invasive where a woman was concerned.

Detailed crime scene photos were taken, autopsies were performed in the house, and the stomach contents were examined, but forensic science was in its infancy. Fingerprints, hair and fiber samples and other modern techniques were, for the most part, still in the realm of science fiction.

Two days later, Lizzie was seen burning a dress (she claimed was covered in brown paint) in the kitchen stove. About a week later she was formally arrested. The police declared that her motive for the grisly murders had been money. Her trial was conducted the following June. Generally, the prosecution presented a weak and ineffectual case, while Lizzie's lawyers set about earning their astronomical fees (she paid one lawyer a whopping $25,000!). After a two-week trial, it took the jury only an hour to return their verdict of not guilty. Without the murder weapon or any bloodstained clothing, there was simply not enough evidence to convict.

Soon after the trial, Lizzie and Emma bought a beautiful home in one of the best neighborhoods. Lizzie called the house Maplecroft, and she also changed her own name to Lizbeth. (In 1905, Emma moved to New Hampshire and lived under an assumed name.) Although Lizzie was now a free and wealthy woman, she was ostracized from society. Regardless of what the jury had concluded, many people in Fall River believed she was guilty.

Defiant to the end, Lizzie lived her life in a manner that shocked her peers—consorting with theater people, throwing wild parties, and possibly even having an affair with an openly gay actress. She died in 1927 after complications from gall bladder surgery, and left most of her money to animal rescue organizations. Emma died nine days later from injuries sustained after falling down a staircase. Bridget moved to Montana, married, and had an ordinary life. There were reports she was about to make a deathbed confession, but then recovered. She died in 1948.

If Lizzie had been innocent, she spent the rest of her life being cruelly punished for something she didn't do. If, however, she had swung that ax, or helped the person who did, she got away with one of the boldest and bloodiest murders of the nineteenth century.

All of the people involved went silently to their graves, but one question still remains—have any of them returned to the scene of the crime?

In 1994, Martha McGinn inherited the Borden house from her grandparents. They had lived in the house for over forty years, and during that time, windows would open and close by themselves, lights would turn on and off, and objects seemed to travel from room to room on their own. For example, many evenings, Martha would put a book on her bed, get changed into her nightclothes, and then find the book was gone. The books were later found as far away as the basement.

The basement does seem to be a particularly active part of the house, and it was here that one of the most remarkable incidents occurred. While doing some chores, Martha looked up and watched in amazement as an apparition of a woman dressed in Victorian clothing walked across the room in the back of the basement and disappeared into a smaller room, which was once used for firewood storage. The apparition made no attempt to communicate, and did not appear threatening in any manner, but it nonetheless made a lasting impression on Martha!

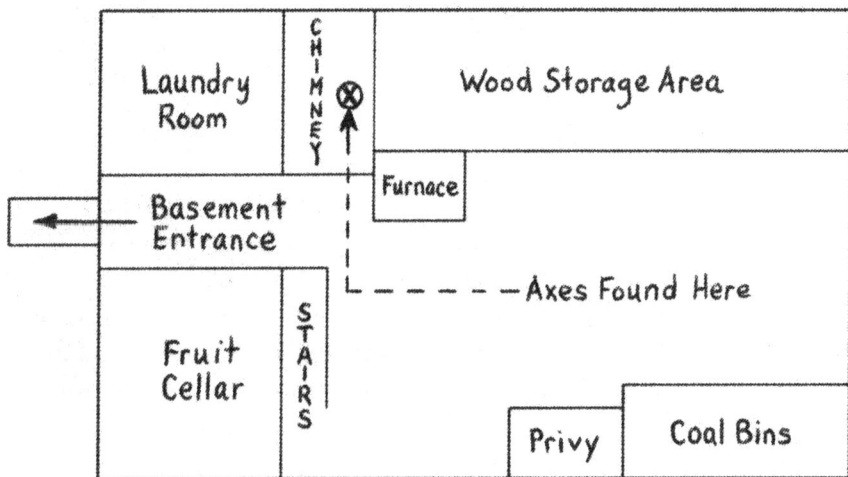

The floor plan of the basement as it was in 1892. (Please note: Floor plans are not drawn to scale.) A box of axes was found in a chimney, and one with a broken handle was used as an example during the trial.

Soon after the house was opened as a bed and breakfast in 1996, members of the staff reported seeing other ghostly figures in the basement. One psychic who visited the house claimed that she felt the murderer was a man who entered the house through the basement, and left the same way.

However, except for the alleged decapitation of the cat, no known acts of violence can be attributed to the basement.

Then what attracts these spirits to the basement? Perhaps the crimes were planned there, or perhaps evidence was hidden or destroyed in some dark corner. (Several times on the day of the murders, police allowed Lizzie to carry her chamber pot down to the basement by herself, and empty it into the privy, as no Victorian gentleman would dare to examine a woman's chamber pot!) Or, the spirits could simply be capable of walking the entire house, from the dark basement up to the third floor.

Some spirits may even walk in what used to be the Borden's yard. In the print shop that is connected to the Borden house, some employees have seen ghostly figures near the printing press. Where the press is now located was the side yard of the Borden property in 1892. Was something buried beneath that spot, or are the spirits just curious about the print shop and the people who work there?

Another puzzling phenomena that occurs on a somewhat regular basis is the sound of children playing marbles on the floor. The sound of glass marbles rolling across the hardwood floor is unmistakable. Of course, there are a few slight problems—no children are in the house when the sound is heard, and the floors in the rooms contain wall to wall carpeting!

The origins of this seemingly innocent haunting activity are possibly quite sinister. It seems that the Bordens weren't the only people to be murdered on Second Avenue in Fall River. A neighbor murdered her children and threw their bodies into the well. A psychic believes that the spirits of these children have taken up residence in the Borden house.

The most active and frightening room may be the John Morse room, where Lizzie's uncle spent the night before the murders, and where Abby was killed. It is definitely always the coldest room in the house, with many people reporting a particularly icy area over the exact spot of Abby's murder.

One morning an employee, Kerri, cleaned the Morse room and made the bed. She was just about to leave when she turned and saw an impression on the bedspread. This was strange, because she had just finished smoothing out the sheets and bedspread. Then she realized the impression was in the exact shape of a human form, as if an adult was lying on the bed with its head on the pillow and its legs stretched out almost the length of the bed. The only problem was that this adult was invisible.

Kerri ran out of the room, and Martha appropriately described her as being "white as a ghost." Kerri would not only never step foot in the Morse room again, she refused to ever step back into the house—not even to pick up her paycheck!

82

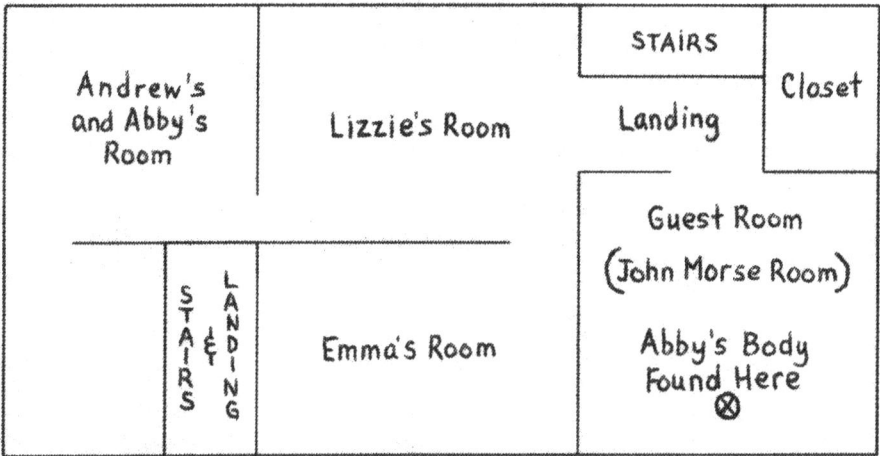

The floor plan for the second floor. (Note the lack of hallways.) Today, the guest bedroom where Abby was murdered is known as the John Morse room.

Abby's body was found on the floor here, next to the bed. I took this photo soon after arriving at the Borden house. When the photos were developed, I noticed the round bright spot on the pillows. In the color original, it is clear that this white light was not caused by my finger or camera strap in front of the lens, but I can not explain what it is.

Not all of the paranormal activity in the Lizzie Borden house is frightening. In fact, one incident was actually helpful, and may have

83

prevented serious injuries, or death. As light bulbs in the house have a habit of burning out prematurely, it is not unusual to have to replace bulbs on a regular basis. One day a member of the staff, Michelle, was precariously perched on the second floor landing, leaning over the banister replacing a bulb from the fixture over the staircase. She started to lose her balance and was about to plummet to the first floor, when someone grabbed her and prevented her from falling. No one could be seen, but perhaps whomever it was who provided the helping hands had decided the house had seen enough tragedy.

A new type of haunting seems to have begun just recently. Both guests and staff hear a cat meowing and scratching on doors as if wanting to enter a room. There have also been several sightings throughout the house of a cat and a pair of glowing green eyes. As there are no cats living there, could this be Abby's cat, returning to search for its owner who met a similar fate?

One the most dramatic paranormal events was witnessed by employee Eleanor Thibault. For her first eighteen months working at the Lizzie Borden house, nothing strange or inexplicable ever happened to her. That was to change during the winter of 2001, when she was alone in the house waiting for guests to arrive. Eleanor was in the in the sitting room in a chair directly across from the sofa (where Andrew was murdered), reading a good book.

"All of a sudden this strange feeling came over me—an awful feeling that someone was there," Eleanor recalls. "I ran into the kitchen to get the cell phone."

Returning to her chair, she called Martha's mother, Sally, who also works at the house. As the two women spoke, Eleanor saw something coming out of the kitchen doorway, which was to her right. It looked like a cloud of smoke, about one foot thick, and it slowly rolled out of the kitchen near the ceiling. Concerned that there might be a fire, she told Sally what she was seeing, and insisted it must be smoke since it was coming from the kitchen.

However, this distinct patch of white "smoke" moved slowly and deliberately over to the sofa and stopped directly above the spot where Andrew Borden's face and skull had been mutilated with an ax. Then the misty cloud began to dissipate, until it completely disappeared.

"When I saw it disappear I told Sally to never mind and hung up. Then I called Martha to tell her what I had just experienced. I guess it wasn't smoke after all."

Whether you call it ectoplasm, spirit energy or a nebulous apparition, Eleanor was initiated into the Borden house hauntings in a remarkable and memorable fashion. But was it the spirit of Andrew, or Abby, or possibly even the murderer? The awful feeling that preceded the sighting would tend to suggest that it was something of a sinister nature, but the presence of any ghost would be enough to make those who are sensitive feel uncomfortable.

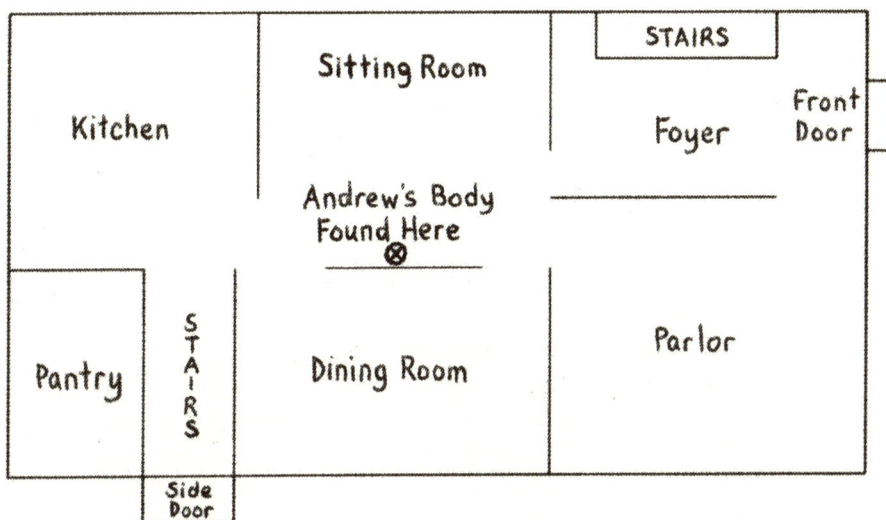

The first floor of the Borden house. Eleanor witnessed the "smoke" leaving the kitchen and moving to the spot where Andrew was murdered.

Unfortunately, that was not to be Eleanor's only paranormal experience. On another occasion she was leading some guests through the sitting room, and she felt a hand press down on her shoulder.

"At first it didn't register, and then I realized no one was near me," Eleanor said. "I didn't scream, although I felt like it. I didn't want to scare the guests so I just kept walking. When I left the room, the hand was gone."

When I interviewed Eleanor in late July, 2002, she indicated that another strange event had just occurred a few days earlier. It was a Saturday night, and she had just started brewing a fresh pot of coffee before conducting the private tour of the house for the guests who were spending the night. The tour generally takes about an hour, so by the time they all returned to the kitchen the coffee should have been piping hot. She poured a few cups and handed them to guests, who quickly discovered the coffee was cold.

This was very unusual, because the restaurant-grade coffee maker had never given any trouble. Eleanor tested the switches and looked for any signs of problems. Everything seemed in order, until she looked at the cord. Sometime after everyone began the tour, and after the coffee had brewed, someone, or something, had pulled the cord out of the socket. The way the coffee maker is positioned on the table with the cord running behind it, there was no way for this to happen accidentally. The freshly made coffee would have needed a considerable amount of time to cool, and no one had left the tour at any time. Just another of the Lizzie Borden house's little mysteries!

Having had a couple of conversations with Sally and Eleanor, I realized this was not a case I could write about simply by interviewing witnesses. The Borden house needed to be experienced—preferably during the anniversary week, when activity is high. The problem would be trying to get a dogsitter on a day that Bob had off, and the Borden house had an open room. It also needed to be much sooner than later, as I wanted to include the story in the new book I was working on, which needed to be completed in a few weeks.

Like some cosmic orchestration, everything suddenly fell into place for Friday, August 9. The company where Bob works was going to be closed that day. Our friend, Barbara Janicki, who dogsits for us, usually is never available on a Friday, as she always watches a friend's baby that day. However, one day as we spoke on the phone, she happened to mention that she would have that entire week off because her friend's family was going on vacation. To complete the orchestration, it also turned out that Mike Worden (police officer and fellow ghost hunter) and his girlfriend, Kelly Montgomery, both had that day off and could join us.

Now all we needed were a couple of rooms. Even though it was the height of the tourist season, the third floor rooms were still available, and we were soon booked and anxious to go.

About a week before our trip, Sally called and said there was someone I should probably interview. She said a couple from Ohio had recently stayed in the Jennings room on the third floor, and the woman, Sara Chinnock, had a startling experience in the middle of the night. A few hours later I spoke to Sara and she told me of her bizarre, and terrifying, encounter.

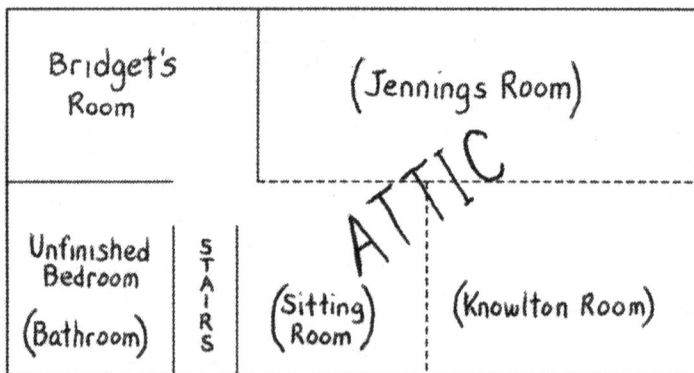

The third floor was where Bridget Sullivan's room was located. The present day Jennings and Knowlton rooms were open attic space in 1892, and the bathroom and sitting room are also recent additions.

Sara Chinnock did not believe in ghosts. When she was growing up her parents had impressed upon her that there was no such thing as a ghost, and that everything had a natural and logical explanation. So when an apparition walked through her room at the Lizzie Borden house, Sara was completely unprepared to deal with the intellectual and emotional impact of the experience.

Sara lives in Ohio, and for several years she has worked as an assistant to a mayor. While she enjoys her job, she also likes to get away and travel with her boyfriend, Chris. Chris believes in ghosts and thought it would be fun to stay in some haunted hotels and B&Bs, so their first trip of this kind was to the Buxton Inn, in Granville, Ohio.

Much to Chris' dismay, their sleep was undisturbed, and nothing went bump in the night. However, a few things were out of the ordinary. The bathroom sink faucet turned itself on. A sturdy mirror that swivels, moved on its own. There were no windows open, no drafts, and the two tried to reproduce the movement by creating a breeze, to no effect. Finally, Sara's camera, which had never given her any problems, refused to rewind in the room. She was afraid she would lose all of her pictures, but when they left, the camera rewound with no problem. While none of these events were convincing enough to convert a lifelong skeptic, Sara began to wonder if everything did have a simple and logical explanation.

When another opportunity to travel came in the summer of 2002, Sara thought it would be nice to go somewhere in New England. She had only been to the region on one other occasion and liked the charm and character of the northeastern states. While looking over some web sites on things to do, she came across information about the Lizzie Borden house. Upon discovering it had been converted into a bed and breakfast, she decided it would be the perfect place to stay—its location would give her the opportunity to soak up some New England flavor, and its violent history and alleged ghosts would give her boyfriend a chance to experience a world famous haunting.

It was a long 13-hour drive from Ohio through Pennsylvania, New York, Connecticut, Rhode Island and finally into Massachusetts. The trip seemed even longer when the car's air conditioning stopped working on that hot and humid first of July. However, it all seemed worthwhile when they checked into the Jennings Room on the third floor, and then enjoyed a private tour of the house that evening.

Their guide, Ed, told the fascinating story of the days leading up to the murders, the gruesome details of the double homicide, and the ensuing trial that captivated the nation. By the time they went to bed, Sara and Chris were full of visions of one the bloodiest and most mysterious crimes in American history. However, they slept through the night without incident, although their second night would be a very different story.

Shortly before bed, Chris decided to recharge his camcorder battery. Inexplicably, the electronics went haywire, and he was afraid something had shorted out. While the camcorder had never acted that way before, his only concern was that it was broken. Neither of them suspected that an unnatural energy might be manifesting in their room.

Waking up several times throughout the night is nothing new for Sara, although usually she just looks at the clock, rolls over and eventually goes back to sleep. When she awoke at about 3am the morning of July 3, there certainly wasn't any reason to be alarmed. Even we she first saw a woman in her room, she wasn't afraid, but that was to change very rapidly.

"There was a figure that was all white, a woman, and she walked away from the bed toward a doorway. She was carrying a tray, and as she was passing through the doorway, she turned and looked directly at me. Then she was gone," Sara told me over the phone, the memory of the recent event still fresh in her mind.

"For a second I thought, 'Oh, a woman with a tray is walking through our room,' but then it hit me. Everything was completely white—her face, her hair, her dress, the tray. Then she went through a partially opened door in a solid part of the wall where there is no door, and both the figure and the doorway vanished."

"I was absolutely terrified, yet at the same time my mind was telling me that this couldn't happen. My mom and dad told me there were no such things as ghosts. It couldn't possibly happen, yet it had just happened."

The figure had been rather tall and thin, with short or upswept hair, and just enough of a bust to distinguish it as a woman. The clothing appeared to be old-fashioned, but the dress did not reach to the floor—simply because there were no feet to be seen as the figure moved above the floor. The apparition held the tray level in front of her with two hands, as if something was balanced on top of it, although Sara didn't notice anything on it. And despite all of the detail she was able to see, the figure had no discernable face.

Sara sat in the darkness in silent terror for several minutes. She desperately wanted to awaken Chris, but he was sleeping soundly and she didn't want to frighten him. Sara was also still wrestling with the concept of what she had just seen. Rather than shake him awake, she moved restlessly around for almost twenty minutes. Finally Chris awoke and asked in a groggy voice if everything was okay.

Sara now had the chance to tell of her experience, but she found that she was still so shaken she couldn't speak. Instead, she began to cry, and only after she had let it all out emotionally, could she begin to tell Chris what had happened. He was very sympathetic and suggested they pack up and leave right away. Instead, they got dressed and went outside to smoke a cigarette and talk about it some more.

"We could have left right away, but as I stood outside I realized that this was what we had paid for. This was why we had come all that way. We eventually went back up to the room, but neither of us slept anymore that night."

Another thing that entered into their decision to stay was the fact that although Sara had been completely terrified, she never felt as if the figure was in any way threatening. Also, somewhat ironically, while Sara stated that there was "a certain energy to the house," she did not sense it in the Jennings Room.

Mercifully, their third and final night at the Lizzie Borden house was apparition-free. They both had trouble sleeping, but that is perfectly understandable in lieu of the previous night's visitor.

And who could this visitor have been? From the description of the physical characteristics, it is unlikely it was any of the Borden women. However, the maid, Bridget Sullivan had been taller, and a servant would be the most likely person to be carrying a tray. Finally, the Jennings Room is on the third floor, adjacent to the room in which Bridget lived at the time of the murders, and indeed the very room in which she had claimed to be in at the actual time of the murders.

If this was the spirit of the Borden's maid, is there any significance to her appearing with a tray in the third floor room, which at the time of the murders was simply attic storage space? Or did she appear in that manner just to identify herself as a servant, and make it known that she has not left the premises? Perhaps it is some kind of guilt that keeps her locked to that house—the guilt of knowing more about the murders of her employers than she divulged to the authorities.

As for Sara, I asked how this experience had changed her life. She replied that she now has to reevaluate her experiences and beliefs, and despite the sheer terror of the ghost in her bedroom, she is curious to visit other haunted locations. She wants to see if this was a once-in-a-lifetime occurrence, or if she is actually sensitive to this other world she has so recently discovered. Perhaps the most important thing to come out of this, however, is the fact that her teenaged daughter thinks her mother's experience was really cool!

At the end of the interview, Sara asked if I would get in touch with her after our stay at the Lizzie Borden house. I told her I would be happy to tell her all about it, if there was anything to tell…

As I write these words, I am sitting in the gazebo in our yard on the hot Sunday morning of August 11, 2002. Birds are chirping, butterflies are touching down softly on the few flowers left during this drought-plagued summer, and sun-drenched woods are only a few feet away. In this tranquil setting, it is almost impossible to imagine that just yesterday I was in Lizzie Borden's house. And it is laughable that just a few days ago I wrote about Sara's experiences and concluded that I would get in touch with her "if there was anything to tell." Little did I know that we were going to experience things that no other guests had in the six years that the house has been operating as a bed and breakfast.

I was up at 5am on the morning of Friday, August 9, which is only half an hour earlier than I usually get up. After getting everything packed and ready, I made a quick trip to the wonderful little Goshen Bakery (with my dogs, who would ride in cars all day if given the chance) to buy a supply of goodies for Barbara, our dogsitter. I had been telling her about their donuts and fritters for years, and bought enough to keep her happy for the rest of the weekend.

Bob and I were soon headed up the coast on Route 95 in Connecticut— otherwise known as the Highway of Neverending Construction. Stopping at a rest stop in Rhode Island, I noticed that almost the entire top rack of brochures had at least one Lizzie Borden picture on them. Fall River, Massachusetts has a gold mine because of Lizzie, and they are not shy about publicizing her. (One shudders to think if in one hundred years there will be an O.J. Simpson Bed and Breakfast!?)

Fall River sits on a beautiful section of land looking down on the Taunton River. When you drive through the historic Highlands section with its stately homes and mansions, it's easy to picture the wealthy citizens of Lizzie's era riding in their carriages to attend sumptuous dinner parties surrounded by all that pre-income tax America had to offer. It's also easy to understand why Lizzie was considerably ticked off about living in the Borden's humble home—far removed from the glamour and luxury her father could have easily afforded.

After a quick lunch, we went to the Historical Society of Fall River, which is in the magnificent former Brayton House. The structure began its existence down the hill in 1843. When a wealthy local man named Remington decided he wanted a stone home, he bought the structure in 1870, gutted the interior, disassembled the stones, and had them reconstructed on a prime piece of property in the Highlands. Sparing no expense on a new interior, the house became a showpiece of black walnut doors and moulding, stenciled ceilings, etched glass, and countless paintings and decorative objects—not to mention the hot and cold running water and flush toilets. The real piece de resistance came in 1877, when a temporary structure was added to house the 500 guests for his daughter's wedding.

Perhaps due in part to this extravagance, Remington's depleted finances forced him to sell his lovely home to the Braytons, and it was one of their descendants who donated the house to the Historical Society in the early twentieth century. I mention this brief history of the house and urge you to visit for two reasons—it is Victorian gem and shows everything that Lizzie was missing, and it now houses the largest collection of artifacts, documents and photos related to the murders and trial.

The last room on the house tour contains such unique items as bits of the stomach contents removed from Andrew and Abby during their autopsies, and the hairpiece Abby was wearing when she was killed. There are murder scene photos, clothing worn by Lizzie, and other fascinating pieces of Borden-abilia. In the Society's extensive collection of all things Lizzie, they even have replicas of the shattered skulls, which had been made before the originals were returned to Andrew and Abby's bodies.

(An interesting side note: For evidence for the trial, the prosecution had Mr. and Mrs. Borden's heads cut off from their bodies. The heads were then boiled in water in order to strip off all of the flesh. The cleaned skulls were produced in court to show how a hatchet found in the Borden basement neatly fit into the gaping wounds. When these skulls were unveiled during the trial, Lizzie fainted, and probably gained considerable sympathy from the jury.

Recently, someone with ground penetrating radar discovered that the men who were paid to place the skulls back with the bodies might not have completed their tasks. It appears as if, rather than opening the caskets and putting the skulls in their rightful places, they were simply tossed on top of the lids and recovered with dirt. If ever two spirits had good cause to not rest in peace, it would be Andrew and Abby!

Toward the end of our tour, I heard one of the clocks strike four. That was check-in time at the Lizzie Borden B&B, and I wanted to get there right away as I had arranged to interview some of the staff. About twenty minutes later, we pulled into the driveway of the Borden house. I told Bob to wait while I checked in and found out if it was okay to leave the van there. The front door was locked, and no one answered when I knocked. I shrugged my shoulders toward Bob as I walked back past the van, and then tried the side door. That was unlocked, and I could see down he hall into the kitchen. I called out "hello" several times, with no response. Finally, I went inside and found several people in the sitting room (where Andrew was murdered).

I asked if this was the place to check in, and they said it was, but that no one was there. I asked for some clarification, and was told that they had been let into the house by two women from the adjacent museum and office. Those women said the hostess would be there in a few minutes and then they left. That had been an hour and a half ago.

The guests included: Julia Bayless of Toluca, Illinois, and her daughters Amanda and Michelle Gerdes, Judy and Dave Payton of Hastings on Hudson, New York, and Angela Franks and Heather Kingsbury of Brooklyn, Michigan. Mike Worden and Kelly Montgomery had been delayed in traffic, but arrived about half an hour later.

I told Bob to come inside and then started to look for some kind of contact list of staff members. The other guests had already searched the house and hadn't found anything, and just continued to sit and wait. Waiting is something I do not do very well. And I was concerned about the woman who was supposed to be there. I had spoken to her a couple of weeks earlier, and knew that if she were able to get to a phone, she would have let someone know that she was delayed.

Two hours passed and there was still no word. Had another violent act been committed in the Lizzie Borden house, and could the perpetrator still be hiding somewhere inside? Or had there been an accident, and precious minutes were ticking by?

I knew that at home I had written down the phone numbers of two of the staff members to whom I had spoken. Using my cell phone, I called Barbara and asked if she wouldn't mind going upstairs to my office to look for them. I hated to ask, because she had a broken foot and stairs were not the easiest things for her to climb at that point. However, I waited as she slowly made it up to my office and began to search for the numbers.

I keep a spiral notebook by the phone to jot down names, phone numbers and information, and I knew that the Lizzie Borden numbers should be right at the top of a recent page. She searched for several minutes but couldn't find them. I thanked her for trying and then shut off my phone. A minute later, she found the numbers, but couldn't reach me because my phone was off!

As we waited, we struck up various conversations with the other guests in the parlor and sitting room. We found that Julia and her daughters had been on quite a trip which had taken them from Illinois, to Gettysburg, PA, to Salem, MA, and finally to the Lizzie Borden house. They were on kind of an unofficial ghost tour and were looking forward to some investigating that night.

Angela told us that when she first went up to the second floor, she heard a woman crying. Walking toward the sound of the crying, she found that it was coming from the John Morse room, which had been the guest room where Abby was murdered. The crying stopped when she entered the room, but began again when she walked away. No one else was on the second floor at the time.

Dave had worked the night before and therefore had yet to sleep, so he was content to sit in a comfortable chair in the sitting room and try to catch a few winks, but Judy was clearly into the moment as we all exchanged stories. She said that her friends had joked that Lizzie didn't want her to visit, because her computer had refused to print directions to the house. Also, her new car (on which she had only made three payments) was found to have a broken axle just the week before the trip. Then, they finally arrived at the house and no one was there.

It was fascinating how eleven strangers came together in an empty murder house and were having a great time! However, as time continued to pass, I knew something had to be done. I called the local police and informed them that there were guests in the Borden house, but no staff. I was not requesting that they come to the house, I simply hoped they would know who to contact. At first the officer thought it was a rather a funny situation, until I told him the house was unlocked and the hostess had been missing for hours. He said they would immediately look into it.

A few minutes later there was a loud, persistent knocking on the front door. It was Fall River police officer David St. Laurent, who had only been a few blocks away when he got the call. Two other police officers were quickly on the scene and the three of them searched the house from top to bottom. They, too, were concerned that there had been foul play. Perhaps for the first time since the day of the Borden murders in 1892, police were searching the house for victims and trying to solve a mystery!

There was definitely tension in the air as they looked for the missing woman, and the fact that it was the Lizzie Borden house multiplied the feeling many times over. However, they found nothing—nothing living, that is.

As Officer St. Laurent entered the basement, he heard shuffling footsteps by the far wall—footsteps that moved away as he got closer. Then he saw a coffin containing a body. Was this a victim? Was this someone's idea of a joke? Or was this some sick, twisted person who had broken into the house, done something horrible to the hostess and was now lying in wait for another victim? St. Laurent received no response from the person when he asked it to identify itself. Thrusting his gun forward into the coffin and again demanding a response, he saw that the figure was missing its head, and that it was nothing more than a dummy!

When he came upstairs, he told us the story and we all had a really good laugh. It turned out that this was nothing more than a Halloween prop they stored in the basement, but considering this was the basement of an ax murder house and the hostess was missing, his caution is understandable. The fact that he stood his ground alone, is commendable. However, while the figure in the coffin was explained, the footsteps he heard remain a mystery, as no one else was in the basement at the time.

Although the humorous incident temporarily relieved the tension, the fact remained that the hostess was now missing for almost three hours. I directed one of the policemen to the office and said I had not wanted to go through the desks or papers looking for phone numbers, but as he began searching one desk, I took a look at the papers posted on the walls. Finally, I found a calendar near the front door that had a list of names and phone numbers, with one name I recognized.

I called the officer over, and told him to phone Sally, as I knew she would know what to do. It was somewhat amusing as the officer tried to explain that there were eleven guests and three police officers sitting in the house, and no staff. It was clear the news came as quite a shock, but he assured her the police would remain until the owners arrived. Finally there was hope that we would get to the bottom of this mystery!

When I went back into the house, Officer St. Laurent was keeping everyone entertained by telling stories about the history of Fall River. There could easily have been eleven frightened and agitated guests, but he was the right man for the moment and everyone remained in good spirits. It was, after all, quite an adventure, but there was still the concern for the missing woman.

At this point, two of the police officers left, the other guests decided to go out for dinner, and Bob and I remained to hold down the fort with Officer St. Laurent. Staff member Diane Travers soon arrived, and allayed our fears by telling us there had simply been a very unusual mix-up, due to a personal situation with the woman who had been scheduled to be there. In the six years since the Borden house had been operating as a bed and breakfast, this was the one and only time anything like this had ever happened. Sally had warned me that strange things went on during the anniversary week of the murder, but in my wildest work of fiction I never would have conceived of this! It was like being trapped in some bizarre reality television show, with some potentially very serious consequences.

About fifteen minutes later, owner Martha McGinn arrived, and looked relieved to see that the situation was under control. We all talked for a while, but I was clearly in need of some rest after the long day and all the excitement. Bob and I brought our luggage and equipment to our third-floor Jennings room, but then he decided to go back downstairs to the parlor.

Propping up the pillows on the bed, I stretched out on the comfortable mattress and took a deep breath. At last, I could relax! Until about two minutes later when I thought I heard footsteps in the hallway and sitting room outside my door. It was probably Diane, or Mike and Kelly returning from dinner, I thought. And even if it was a ghost, I was far too tired to care at that moment.

However, the footsteps and creaking continued, and several times it sounded like someone was approaching our room, but the footsteps stopped when they reached the door. If this was someone's idea of a joke, I was not amused. If it was Diane or some guests, I wanted to know what they were doing. It if was something else, I had to know.

Getting up from the bed, I opened the latch, pulled open the door and looked out. Mike and Kelly's room was still empty, and no one was in the sitting room. Going down the hall I found that the bathroom and Bridget's room were also empty, and no one was on the stairs. Still more tired than curious, I went back into our room and made sure the latch was securely closed. It is an old fashioned type of latch where you need to firmly press down a lever in order to raise an iron bar out of a slot. It is not the type of mechanism that could possibly open on its own. Or so I thought.

About a minute after I climbed back into bed, the footsteps began again. Then I heard the distinctive clinking sound of the lever being depressed and the bar snapping out of the slot, and the door swung open about eight inches. I expected to see the door continue to open and Bob walk in. The door stopped and no one was there.

Bob and I have a deal that we never play jokes during an investigation, and I couldn't believe he would pull anything like this now, in the Lizzie Borden house of all places. Literally leaping out bed this time, I swung open the door and said, "Bob, this isn't funny!" There was no response. I hurried to the other rooms and found no one. I called down the stairs and there was silence. Apparently, someone was very curious about me and wanted to get my attention. Phantom footsteps and opening my door was a sure way to accomplish that.

Stubborn to the core, and still tired, I hoped they had had their fun and would now let me get a little rest. Once again I climbed back into bed and when nothing happened for a minute or two I began to settle down. Then there were more footsteps clearly climbing the staircase to the third floor. They entered the sitting room and came straight for my door. Jumping out of bed, I yanked open the door with a serious look of determination on my face. There stood Mike and Kelly, looking at me wondering what was my problem.

I asked if they had been up here in the past few minutes, and they said that they had just now returned from dinner. I asked if they knew where Bob was, and they said he was on the first floor still chatting with everyone. All of the other guests were still out to dinner. I had been the only person on either the second or third floor when I heard the footsteps and had my door opened.

I explained what had just happened, and Mike and I tried to find some possible explanation. I remained in the room and shut the door. Mike pressed his weight against the door and it didn't budge. He even partially depressed the lever on the outside and then leaned against the door again, and still it wouldn't open. The lever must be pressed completely down with a firm push in order to raise the bar on the inside, out of its slot. Thus, the police officer and the ghost investigator thereby officially confirmed that the door could not have opened on its own!

It was now clear I wasn't going to get any real rest, but I went back to bed anyway, and at least gave it a shot. Bob came up about fifteen minutes later and said that our tour would begin soon. I told him that my tour had already begun, and he swore he had not been upstairs before. He also tested the latch and concluded it could not accidentally pop open.

The latch on the Jennings Room door. The lever on the outside must be depressed completely in order for the bar to rise out of the slot.

I threw on some comfortable old sweat pants, got my gear together and we headed downstairs. Everyone was still buzzing from our afternoon's adventure, and anxious to get started with the tour. I told everyone about the footsteps and my door opening itself. Mike came downstairs and said that both the light in his room and Bridget's room went on and off several times by themselves. It seemed like everyone, living and dead, was ready to go.

I asked Diane if she minded if I used my tape recorder so I wouldn't miss anything, and she said it was fine. Apparently, however, it was not fine with the spirits of the Lizzie Borden house, because the tape recorder kept turning itself on and off the entire time we were on the first floor. When we reached the second floor there was no problem. Only one other time (see page 2) had this tape recorder acted that way, and if there had been something wrong with it, or the batteries were low, there was no reason for it to correct itself on the second floor.

Diane was an excellent tour guide. She gave us the blow-by-blow details (so to speak) of the murders, and what was happening in each room just prior, during and after the crimes. The story was chilling in itself, but to be standing on the exact spots where the murderer swung the ax into the heads of Andrew and Abby Borden's heads, was so intense as to be surreal. It is a spine-tingling sensation, regardless of whether or not you believe in ghosts. Even if nothing strange ever occurred in the one hundred and ten years following the murders, the Lizzie Borden house would still be one of the most frightening locations you could ever visit.

Naturally, in addition to the usual facts surrounding the case, I was interested in the paranormal end of the spectrum. Diane obliged by pointing out what sightings had occurred in what locations. For example, one couple on their honeymoon spent the night in the John Morse room. In addition to being a really strange choice as a place to spend your honeymoon, the newlyweds were subjected to more than they bargained for.

Perhaps if Abby's restless spirit does still dwell in the room where she was brutally murdered, she did not appreciate the amorous nature of the couple's visit. They claimed that the bed lifted off of the floor (not as the result of their honeymoon activities) and shoes and other objects were thrown across the room. Without telling anyone, they packed and left in the middle of the night, only later explaining to the staff what had happened. Probably not coincidentally, on a separate occasion, another honeymooning couple left that room (and the house) suddenly in the middle of the night, and the staff never did find out why.

Diane admitted that when she first began working at the house three years ago, she wouldn't step foot into the Morse room. She conducted that part of the tour from the doorway. She will now enter the room, but if she has to spend the night there, she will turn some of the pictures toward the wall and remove some items before trying to go to sleep.

In Lizzie's room, I asked if anything unusual had happened during the previous weekend, which was the anniversary of the murders. Both Eleanor and Sally had mentioned that strange things often happen throughout that week (which was why we were there on Friday of that week). She said that during a tour, she went to open Lizzie's door and it was locked—from the inside! They never lock doors during a tour, and she had to go downstairs, up the back staircase and through Andrew and Abby's room to open the door.

Also, the cash register in the print shop was malfunctioning, items were found in different rooms from where they had been placed, and several lights blew out. It did indeed seem that the week of August 4 was full of surprises.

When we all gathered in Andrew and Abby's room, Diane told the story of the phantom cat (or what I have come to call "Abby's Tabby"). It was not until the next morning that Amanda, who does not believe in ghosts, told us that as Diane spoke, she heard a soft sound like something landing on the bed. She looked over and saw a grayish striped cat with four white paws standing on the bed. It immediately jumped to the floor, walked past her mother and disappeared. At the time she was certain it was only the power of suggestion, since Diane was at that moment talking about the cat ghost, but her sister Michelle had heard a cat meowing when they first arrived that afternoon, so perhaps she should believe her own eyes.

The tour continued up to the third floor rooms, where several people tested the latch on our door, and examined the area around Lizzie's sewing machine where Sara Chinnock saw the apparition of the maid (and where she also thought she saw a pair of green eyes). Then it was down to the basement where we all once again had a good laugh imagining Officer St. Laurent confronting the dummy in the coffin.

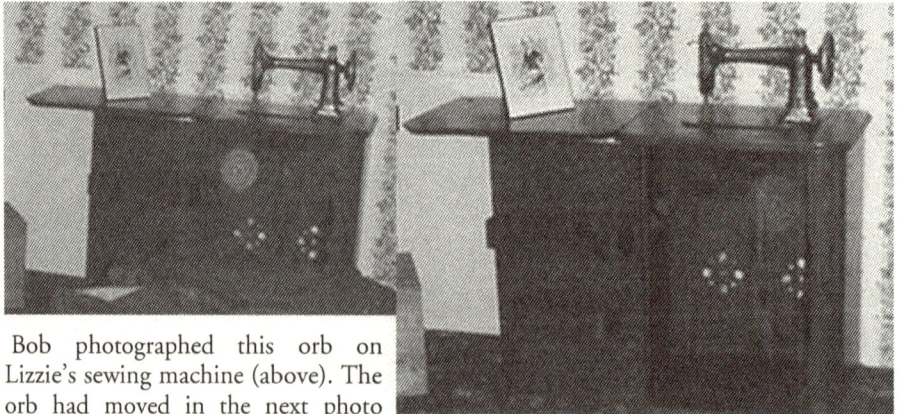

Bob photographed this orb on Lizzie's sewing machine (above). The orb had moved in the next photo (right), taken a few seconds later.

Everyone gathered around the coffin for a group photo. From left to right: Bob, Angela, Diane, Amanda, Heather, Michelle, Julia, Mike, Judy, Dave and Kelly.

Once the official tour ended, it was time for the real investigation to begin. Our first stop was the basement. Mike and I both set up our camcorders facing the area where Martha had once seen a woman in Victorian clothing walk into the old wood storage room and disappear. Bob turned out the lights, we switched to infrared and almost immediately I began to see those little white lights zipping from where we were standing into the old wood room. There were quite a few, mostly headed from our direction away from us, but there were also several that came from the opposite wall toward us. We didn't feel the slightest breeze, and even if there was a draft, it is doubtful that dust or particles would be bouncing back and forth in straight lines at such a high rate of speed.

Mike also photographed several orbs near the Halloween coffin, and Bob captured one by the basin in the old chimney. It was impossible to get any accurate EMF readings, as everywhere I turned there seemed to be another circuit box or electrical line. Readings were high everywhere, but the normal electrical current would account for that. When we went upstairs and showed everyone the footage, I suggested that Julia, Michelle and Amanda use the infrared feature on their camcorder and see what they got. A little while later they returned, having taped the same strange moving objects.

Judy and Dave were nice enough to let us set up the camcorders in their room (the Morse room) for a while. I especially appreciated it since Dave still hadn't had a chance to catch any sleep. There wasn't too much activity, but Bob did tape one large bright object that seemed to slowly rise off the floor (on the spot where Abby had been murdered), float sideways past the camcorder and out of sight. When we played that section of the tape back for

99

everyone, it was funny to hear Bob's running commentary, which was essentially, "Oooh, ooh, oooooooh!"

After turning out lights in and around the sitting room, we began taping there. The camcorders were both aimed at the sofa where Andrew got whacked, and for quite a while there wasn't anything to be seen. Just as I concluded that nothing was going to happen, a few plump little orbs passed back and forth over the sofa.

As exciting and unique an opportunity as this investigation was, it was getting very late and I was dead on my feet. My last act for the night was to set up the camcorder in our room, aimed toward the corner where the ghostly maid had appeared. Then we went to bed.

The tape ran for about an hour and a half, and in the days after I returned from our trip, I had the rather monotonous task of watching the footage. If nothing is happening, then you are essentially sitting and staring at the wall for approximately the length of a feature film. At first, however, I was encouraged, because within minutes of starting the camera, there appeared to be a few of those little white darting lights, but then nothing. And more nothing.

I watched the tape about twenty to thirty minutes at a time—otherwise your eyes begin to play tricks on you staring at the same scene for prolonged periods. Several times I had to rewind and play back sections, thinking I had seen something moving. Watching it in fast forward is no good, either, because the quality is greatly diminished and you could easily miss something crucial.

With only a few minutes of tape left, I was tempted to just say the heck with it, when something caught my eye. It looked as though something floated in front of the camcorder. But it was late, and I had been watching for almost half an hour, so I couldn't be sure that I could trust my eyes. Pressing the rewind button for a second, I let it go and moved closer to the screen. Sure enough, there was a small, hazy patch, perhaps the size of a golf ball, which moved from the edge of the bed and continued toward the wall before it disappeared from the camcorder's field of view.

I called to Bob to come and look. He clearly saw it too, but he also noticed that it first came into view over the bed, right in front of where he was sleeping. The object didn't seem to have any particular agenda, it just floated slowly on a fairly level plain just above the level of the bed, out over the floor, and either dissipated or simply passed beyond the range of the wide-angle lens.

With renewed interest, I continued watching the remainder of the tape. With less than five minutes left, there was a distinct tapping sound. It's impossible to tell where in the room it originated, but the camcorder's microphone clearly recorded it. Now I was really filled with anticipation. Perhaps the spirit activity was just getting started for the night! Then the tape ran out.

Now, I regret not putting in a fresh tape. In my half-sleeping state, I did hear the camcorder shut off as the tape ran out, but if you have ever been so tired you wouldn't move even if a freight train was headed your way, then you understand why I didn't get up.

I did wake up with a start several times during the night, but after finding no outward cause, I thought I could chalk it up to the excitement of the place and the unusual surroundings. The next morning, however, Mike said that a loud sound woke him up about 4am. Sometime later, Kelly was physically "jostled" awake. She sat up and looked over at Mike, wondering why he had awakened her, but he was fast asleep. Kelly does not believe in ghosts, yet she has to admit it definitely felt as if someone had made physical contact and had shaken her awake.

The next morning Bob and I went down to the sitting room early to check out some of the tapes they have on the murder and trial. Sally arrived, and we sat and talked for a while. We both agreed that although many inexplicable things occur in the house, none of them feel threatening. I have been in enough haunted places to know when a ghost is hell-bent on causing harm, and thankfully, the Lizzie Borden house does not appear to be one of those places.

At 8am, we all gathered in the dining room where Mrs. Borden's autopsy had taken place, and where the killer most likely first stood as the ax reached out to strike Mr. Borden in the face, as he napped on the sofa by the doorway between rooms. Dave, who had spent the night, provided us with a lovely breakfast on the actual table that had belonged to Lizzie when she lived at Maplecroft. In addition to several delicious traditional breakfast items, everyone had to sample a Johnny cake (an extremely bland little pancake of cornmeal and water), which Mr. and Mrs. Borden had eaten the morning of the murders. Lizzie had only eaten sugar cookies for breakfast, so sugar cookies are also part of the breakfast menu—with an amusing twist. The cookies on the platter Dave presented were all cut in the shapes of little axes!

After breakfast it was already time to check out and hit the road. All too suddenly, our adventure was at an end. However, there was still one essential stop to make—the cemetery. After entering the stately stone archway of Oak Grove Cemetery, you immediately see an arrow painted on the pavement. Rather than have hundreds of confused tourists traipsing over the landscape, the owners were wise enough to paint a series of these arrows leading straight to everyone's prime objective—the Borden family graves.

Even with all that had transpired, both Lizzie and Emma had requested to be buried at their father's feet (which is probably just about where his well-traveled skull is today!). This also meant they would lie at the feet of their stepmother, as she is buried by her husband's side, but that couldn't be avoided. Also lying in the family plot are the first Mrs. Borden (Lizzie and Emma's real mother), and little Alice, who died at the age of two before Lizzie was born.

Standing at their graves, even in the bright, hot sun of an August morning, it is still very mysterious, if not just a little spooky, too. If the dead could speak clearly to us, what stories would these spirits have to tell!

Would the miserly Andrew Borden express regret for having thrown women and children out on the street for being a day late on their rent? Would he admit that he had committed the unspeakable act of incest with his daughter, Lizzie? Would he be able to name the killer who struck at him so savagely that a gaping hole was created where his face had been, or does the identity remain a mystery, even to him?

Abby Borden would surely be able to solve the case for us, for she most likely saw her killer—someone she knew very well, because she made no attempt to shield herself from the first blow of the ax. What answers would she provide as to the motives of her killer? Was it money, revenge, or something much darker? If Lizzie had been the victim of her father's abuse, did Abby know about it, and would she forgive Lizzie for an act to which she had been driven?

Lizzie's real mother lies silently there, too. Is her spirit also unable to rest in peace, knowing what had befallen her family? Does she feel guilt for having died so young, believing that if she had lived none of this would have happened?

Emma Borden did not have to wait long to be placed by her sister's side—dying only nine days after Lizzie. Was death a relief to her, so she would no longer have to hold back some terrible secret? Was she loyal to her sister to the bitter end, or had she known that Lizzie actually was innocent?

Then there is the simple curved stone that only bears the name Lizbeth. Could casual passersby ever conceive of what secrets are buried here beneath their feet? Is this the grave of an innocent woman, vilified by the press, shunned by society and unjustly haunted by another's crimes until she drew her last breath on this earth? Or, as you stand there, are you only six feet away from the skeletal arm that gleefully, and repeatedly swung an ax into the faces and heads of her own father and stepmother? Does that very ground contain the decayed remains of one of the most remorseless and brutal murderesses in history?

We now live in a world where we expect instant answers, but unless some new evidence comes to light, the murders of Andrew and Abby Borden will forever remain unsolved. But perhaps Andrew, Abby, Lizzie, Emma and Bridget have been trying to tell the world what happened over a hundred years ago. Perhaps the apparitions, sounds, lights and bizarre activity in the Borden house is their way of trying to communicate their stories to the world of the living.

To be sure, there are strange forces at work in this house. While some scenes of tragic events simply bear a static imprint, the energy in the Lizzie Borden house is decidedly active. From the basement to the third floor, from broad daylight to the dead of night, restless energies can manifest as passing thoughts, or passing apparitions.

Did Lizzie Borden take an ax and give her stepmother nineteen whacks? And when she saw what she had done, did she give her father eleven? In the final evaluation, perhaps it's best if we never do know for sure. A mystery solved is a mystery no more. In this age of instant information, *not* knowing might be the very thing that continues to draw us to Lizzie's story, and to her house.

It is often frustrating conducting ghost investigations where there is no evidence of any tragic events to connect to the haunting activity. With Lizzie's house, however, you hardly know where to begin to try to connect the wealth of paranormal activity with the countless possible tragic scenarios, but who's complaining? Could a ghost investigator ask for a better place to test her detective skills, equipment—and nerve!

Ultimately, it is undeniably a place you must experience in person. Volumes have been written about the murders and trial, but until you stand on the exact locations of the murderer and the murdered in the Borden house, you will never fully appreciate either the mystery, or the horror, of the case.

Spend a night or two at the Lizzie Borden Bed & Breakfast and test your powers of perception—both with your five senses, and your sixth sense. If the house is eager to divulge its secrets, you might be the one to reveal them. But if the experience does become too intense, and ghostly figures appear before your eyes, you won't be the first person to run out of the house in the middle of the night. Just leave a note in the kitchen before you leave, so they won't have to bake so many ax cookies the next morning…

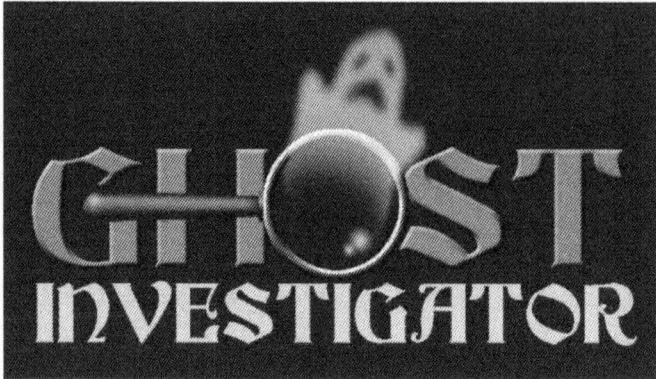

To order books, get info, and share your haunting, contact the Ghost Investigator through:

www.ghostinvestigator.com

Or write to:

Linda Zimmermann
P.O. Box 192
Blooming Grove, NY 10914

Or send email to:

lindazim@frontiernet.net

Copy this page to use for your own ghost hunt. If you know of a haunted site you think should be considered for an upcoming book, please contact me at:
P.O. Box 192, Blooming Grove, NY, 10914
www.ghostinvestigator.com

Field Report

Date: Location:

Time In: Weather:

Names of People Interviewed:

Equipment: Camera ☐ Video ☐ Tape Recorder ☐
                    Thermometer ☐   Other:

Experiences: Sounds ☐ Odors ☐ Cold Spots ☐
    Visuals ☐ Touch/Sensations ☐ Movement ☐

Details (Attach extra sheet if necessary):

Time Out: Total Time on Site:

Conclusions:

Prepared and Signed by:

Witness(es):

Other books by Linda Zimmermann

Look for Linda Zimmermann's new ghost novel in 2003.

Science Fiction Novels

Mind Over Matter   Ten wealthy, powerful members of the Upper Circle rule the Union with an iron fist, and a small chip implanted in every citizen. Born to the privileged class, Walter Danan is now a wanted man. He has discovered extraordinary powers with which he hopes to break the council's grip and set mankind on a higher path of *Mind Over Matter*.
"Classic space opera!" Ernest Lilley, Editor, *SFRevu*

Home Run   On the fast track to becoming a baseball superstar, Rick Stella's injury leads him to join the Pioneer program for a year-long mission. Pioneers are sent into the farthest depths of space to start colonies, and are often never heard from again.

When Rick becomes marooned with his android crew, he must decide whether he is willing to sacrifice his dreams, or risk everything trying to make it home.
"Linda Zimmermann shows why she's an All-star in combining a story about baseball & SF to remind us how to overcome obstacles to emerge a winner!"   Tony Tellado, *Sci-Fi Talk*

History

Civil War Memories "An exciting compilation of vignettes which bring Civil War history alive."   Alan Aimone, USMA West Point

Forging a Nation   "Linda Zimmermann blends the history of a single family with the history of our nation in its formative years. This is a story of patriotism, privilege and tragedy which touches the heart, and gives the reader a fascinating and very personal window into the past."
                          William E. Simon, former U.S. Secretary of the Treasury

"A worthy book." Arthur Schlesinger, Pulitzer Prize winning author/historian

www.ingramcontent.com/pod-product-compliance
Lightning Source LLC
Chambersburg PA
CBHW031323040426
42443CB00005B/199